Deculturalization and the Struggle for Equality

A Brief History of the Education of Dominated Cultures in the United States

SECOND EDITION

Deculturalization and the Struggle for Equality

A Brief History of the Education of Dominated Cultures in the United States

Joel Spring

State University of New York,
College at New Paltz

THE McGRAW-HILL COMPANIES, INC.

New York St. Louis San Francisco Auckland Bogotá Caracas
Lisbon London Madrid Mexico City Milan Montreal New Delhi
San Juan Singapore Sydney Tokyo Toronto

McGraw-Hill

A Division of The McGraw-Hill Companies

This book was developed by Lane Akers, Inc.
This book was set in Palatino by Ruttle, Shaw & Wetherill, Inc.
The editor was Lane Akers;
the production supervisor was Leroy Young.
The cover was designed by Christopher Brady.
The cover photos were provided by Photo Researchers, Inc.
Project supervision was done by Tage Publishing Service, Inc.
R. R. Donnelley & Sons was printer and binder.

DECULTURALIZATION AND THE STRUGGLE FOR EQUALITY
A Brief History of the Education of Dominated Cultures in the United States

This book was printed on acid-free paper.

5 6 7 8 9 0 DOC DOC 9 0 9

ISBN 0-07-060561-0

Library of Congress Cataloging-in-Publication Data

Spring, Joel H.
Deculturalization and the struggle for equality: a brief history of the education of dominated cultures in the United States/Joel Spring.—2nd. ed.
p. cm.
Includes bibliographical references and index.
ISBN 0–07–060561–0
1. Minorities—Education—United States—History.
2. Discrimination in education—United States—History.
3. Segregation in education—United States—History.
4. Multicultural education—United States—History. I. Title.
LC3731.S68 1997 96–19769
371.97'00973—dc20

About the Author

Joel Spring, professor of education at the State University of New York–College at New Paltz, received his Ph.D. in educational policy studies from the University of Wisconsin. His major research interests are history of education, multicultural education, Native American culture, and the politics of education.

Professor Spring is the author of many books including *The Cultural Transformation of a Native American Family and Its Tribe 1763–1995: A Basket of Apples; Images of American Life: A History of Ideological Management in Schools, Movies, Radio, and Television; American Education (now in its seventh edition); Wheels in the Head: Educational Philosophies of Authority, Freedom, and Culture from Socrates to Paul Freire; and the Intersection of Cultures: Multicultural Education in the United States.*

Contents

Preface

In this second edition, I have added a new Chapter 1 on the racial and cultural values brought to North America by English colonists and the early plans for the education of Native Americans. These values help explain Anglo-American bigotry towards Native Americans, African Americans, Asian Americans, and Mexican Americans which resulted in educational discrimination and segregation. In addition, these values, as Ronald Takaki documents in *A Different Mirror: A History of Multicultural America*, are reflected in attempts by the "founding fathers" to ensure that the United States was dominated by an Anglo-American culture.*

The addition of the cultural and racial attitudes of English and Anglo Americans provides a background for a new section in Chapter 1 on early efforts by English colonists and the "founding fathers" to "civilize" Native Americans. These early efforts at "civilizing" Native Americans involved attempts at deculturalization—the destruction of Native American culture—and the replacement of Native American culture with Anglo-American Protestant culture.

In an expanded section on Asian Americans in Chapter 5, I use the discussion of the racial and cultural attitudes of Anglo Americans to help explain the denial of citizenship to Asian immigrants in

*Ronald Takaki, *A Different Mirror: A History of Multicultural America* (Boston: Little, Brown and Company, 1993).

the nineteenth and first half of the twentieth centuries, and the educational segregation of their children.

In Chapter 5, I have added a new section on the current debate about multicultural education. This section demonstrates how the values brought by English colonists to North America still influence current discussions about cultural pluralism.

Similar to the first edition, this book is an adaptation of chapters from my longer study of the history of American education, *The American School, 4th ed.* (McGraw-Hill, 1997).

Deculturalization and the Struggle for Equality

A Brief History of the Education of Dominated Cultures in the United States

CHAPTER 1

Deculturalization and the Racial and Cultural Superiority of Anglo Americans

Deculturalization refers to the stripping away of a people's culture and replacing it with a new culture. This was the method used by the United States government after the conquest of Native Americans. In the nineteenth century, U.S. government leaders and educators rejected the concept of the United States as a multicultural society for a society unified around Protestant Anglo-American culture. In addition, government leaders believed that deculturalization was necessary in order to win the loyalty of conquered Native Americans to the U.S. government. As part of the deculturalization process, federal and state governments instituted programs of Americanization designed to replace native cultures with the dominant white culture of the United States.

In engaging in the act of conquest and the process of deculturalization, the U.S. government reflected a belief held by many Americans in the superiority of Protestant Anglo-American culture and U.S. political institutions. I would argue that most conquering nations justify their actions by claiming cultural and political superiority. In the case of the United States in the nineteenth century, feelings of superiority were embedded in beliefs about the "manifest destiny" of the nation.

Manifest destiny was a belief that ultimately the United States would expand its borders to the Pacific Ocean. Manifest destiny was justified by a belief in the superiority of Protestant Anglo-American culture and U.S. political institutions. Conquered Indian tribes were considered by whites to be culturally and morally inferior. Consequently, educational programs established by the federal government were designed to deculturalize the tribes and then "civilize" them. Deculturalization included attempts to destroy Native American cultures, languages, and religion.

CULTURAL AND RACIAL SUPERIORITY

Feelings of racial and cultural superiority were brought to North America by English colonists in the seventeenth and eighteenth centuries. English colonists arrived in North America with feelings of superiority about their Protestant beliefs and English culture. The invasion of Ireland in the twelfth century initiated a long period of colonial expansion during which the English claimed racial and cultural superiority. From Ireland in the twelfth century to India in the nineteenth century, the English were convinced that colonial expansion was just because it spread Anglo-Saxon culture around the world.

According to historian Ronald Takaki, the English first developed their concepts of racial and cultural superiority during the conquest of Ireland. The English considered the Irish inferior savages who could only be redeemed by adopting English culture. Eventually, English opinion was divided between the possibility of civilizing the Irish and a belief in the innate inferiority of the Irish. The latter position became part of a generalized English belief in their racial superiority.[1]

The English colonizing North America compared their experiences with Indians to their experiences with the Irish. Takaki found many written comparisons during colonial times between the "wild Irish" and the "wild Indians." As with the Irish, English opinion was divided over the possibility of civilizing Native Americans.[2] Extreme racist opinions led to the conclusion that the only solution to the Indian problem was genocide. This attitude is captured in General Philip Sheridan's comment in 1867 after defeating the Cheyennes, "The only good Indians I ever saw were dead." This statement was refined by one of Sheridan's officers to the famous saying, "The only good Indian is a dead Indian."[3]

Also, many Anglo Americans envisioned North America as a land that would be primarily inhabited by whites. Benjamin Franklin worried that there were larger numbers of Africans and

Asians in the world than European whites. He considered expansion into North America an opportunity to increase the white race. Shortly before the American Revolution, as Takaki points out, Franklin argued that the English were the "principle body of white People" that should populate North America. The clearing of the forests, Franklin noted, would serve to make room for more whites. "Why," he asked, "increase the Sons of Africa, by planting them in America, where we have so fair an opportunity, by excluding all Blacks and Tawnys, of increasing the lovely White . . . ?"[4]

Congressional approval of the Naturalization Act of 1790 highlights the racial attitudes of early government leaders. The Naturalization Act excluded from citizenship all nonwhites including *Indians*. Indians were considered domestic foreigners and, therefore, ineligible for citizenship.[5]

In the British colonial empire, English feelings of cultural superiority and racism were used to justify economic exploitation and expropriation of lands. For many European Americans, Indians were an obstacle to the spread of white Europeans from coast to coast. To make room for the expansion of whites, the options were genocide or containment on small farms and reservations. In Takaki's words, "This social construction of race occurred within the economic context of competition over land."[6]

Therefore, English belief in their own cultural and racial superiority over Native Americans and, later, enslaved Africans, Mexican Americans, Puerto Ricans, and Asians, was not born on American soil. It was part of the cultural baggage English colonists brought to North America. English beliefs in their cultural and racial superiority were reinforced by the justifications given for taking over Native American lands. North America acted as a hothouse for the growth of white racism and cultural chauvinism. Again, it is important to stress, that this phenomenon was not unique to North America, but it followed the British flag around the world.

Reflecting the attitudes of English colonists, the "founding fathers" rejected the idea of a multicultural society and advocated the creation of a unified American culture. This new American culture would be formed from Protestant Anglo-Saxon traditions, but an attempt would be made to distinguish this culture from the culture of England. Leading the efforts to create a dominant Protestant Anglo-American culture was the often-called Schoolmaster of America, Noah Webster. Noah Webster worked hard to create a dominant Anglo-

American culture. A prolific writer, he constantly combined efforts to create a dominant culture and build nationalism. An important part of his legacy is a standardized American dictionary of the English language, an American version of the Bible, and his famous spelling book. The wide use of Webster's speller and dictionary throughout the United States created a lasting mold for the American language.[7]

By the 1830s, Noah Webster's dream of a unified national culture continued to be threatened by freed and enslaved Africans, and Native Americans, and, in addition, a new menace appeared in the form of immigrant Irish. The common-school movement of the 1830s and 1840s was, in part, an attempt to halt the drift towards a multicultural society. Self-proclaimed protectors of Anglo-American Protestant culture worried about the Irish immigrants streaming ashore, the growing numbers of enslaved Africans, and the racial violence occurring in northern cities between freed Africans and whites. Also during this period, President Andrew Jackson implemented his final solution for acquiring the lands of the southern Indians which involved forcing them off their lands and removing them to an area west of the Mississippi. Upon completion of this forced removal, the southern tribes were to be "civilized" through a system of segregated schools. In addition to the risk posed to Anglo-American culture, there was a hysterical fear by European Americans during the common-school period that Africans and Indians would contaminate white blood. This fear resulted in a demand by some whites for laws forbidding interracial marriages.

As Carl Kaestle argues in *Pillars of the Republic: Common Schools and American Society, 1780–1860*, public schools in the nineteenth century were primarily designed to protect the ideology of an American-Protestant culture. Most of the common school reformers, he documents, were native-born Anglo-American Protestants, and their public philosophy "called for government action to provide schooling that would be more common, more equal, more dedicated to public policy, and therefore more effective in creating cultural and political values centering on Protestantism, republicanism, and capitalism."[8]

EDUCATIONAL AND CULTURAL DIFFERENCES

When English colonists and later educators and officials of the U.S. government considered deculturalization of Native Americans, they included replacing cultural values related to family structures, gender roles, child-rearing practices, sexual attitudes, economic relationships, and government. Understanding the cultural differences between European Americans and Native Americans provides an indication of what European Americans meant when they talked about "civilizing" Native Americans. The sharp differences in cultural values by those whites who were attracted to the values and lifestyle of Indians and found becoming a "white Indian" a welcome relief from the sexual and economic oppression of white society.[9]

For instance, child-rearing practices were very different between Anglo Americans and Native Americans. New England colonists emphasized discipline, authority, and memorization. Many Anglo Americans believed it was necessary to break the will of the child to assure obedience to, in ascending order, their mother, father, government, church, and God. Corporal punishment was considered a necessary and useful part of child rearing. In fact, they believed that physical punishment was an act of love.

English colonists were appalled at Native American indulgence and permissive attitudes towards their children. Even as late as the 1880s Reverend John Edwards, superintendent of the Wheelock Academy in the Choctaw Nation from 1851 to 1861, was complaining that among Choctaws "there is very little order or discipline in the family. Each does what is pleasing in his own eyes. A parent may beat a child in anger, but seldom does he chastise him with coolness and in love."[10]

In fact, many Europeans and white Americans equated permissiveness in child rearing with different levels of civilization. Indulgence of children indicated to whites a primitive or uncivilized state while strict discipline indicated a high level of civilization. Even as late as the 1920s U.S. anthropologists were arguing, "There is almost a direct ratio between rudeness of culture and gentleness with children."[11]

The education of Native American children did not take place in the formal setting of something called a "school" but it was integrated into the community life of the tribe. The storytelling of elders, the working with adults, the participation in tribal ceremonies and puberty rites, and the customs of the clan and tribe educated Native American children for tribal life.

Use of discipline and authority in child rearing by English colonists was one aspect of what is referred to as the "Protestant ethic." I am using the phrase "Protestant ethic" to mean the following set of values that sharply divided white Anglo-Saxon Protestants from Native Americans.

The Protestant ethic emphasized the importance of hard work and the accumulation of property. Work, among many white Americans, was assumed a good activity that provided protection against sin. Time devoted to work kept the mind from wandering down the path of evil. "Idle hands are the Devil's tools." The Protestant ethic also valued the accumulation of wealth as a sign of God's blessing. In other words, hard work and the accumulation of wealth were considered outward signs of a Godly life.

In contrast, Native Americans believed in the sharing of property. If another tribal member needed food or assistance, others gladly gave their time and food. Most North American tribes did not value the accumulation of property. In addition, there was no concept that work was good in and of itself. In fact, before the introduction of the fur trade there was no reason for a hunter to kill more animals than was needed by the clan. Time not spent hunting or in agricultural pursuits was considered important for celebrations and rituals that linked tribal members to nature and the cosmos. Rather than rushing to work to accumulate property as did most European Americans, Indians appeared to many settlers to be lazy.

Reverend John Edwards reflected the belief of many whites that Native American attitudes about accumulating property and sharing wealth were a major obstacle to their being civilized. "One result of this [sharing wealth]," Edwards admitted in recounting his work with the Choctaws,

> is that they have no need of poorhouses. . . . In fact this unstinted hospitality on one side degenerates into spunging [sic] on the other, the lazy living upon the industrious.
>
> You perceive that this militates very strongly against accumulation of property. . . . To refuse it savors strongly of meanness. But people are learning that it is necessary to refuse, and there is danger that some may go to the opposite extreme.[12]

The Protestant ethic stressed the sacrifice of pleasure for work and wealth. What horrified New England Puritans was that not only did Native Americans seem unconcerned about avoiding personal pleasure, but they also enjoyed sexual pleasure. Since the Christian concept of sin was absent from traditional Indian cultures, tribal members were not driven by a fear of hell to replace personal pleasure with work and accumulation of property. In addition, the lack of a Christian concept of sin regarding sexuality was in sharp contrast with the sexual repression evident among many European Americans. James Axtell provides, as an example of differing attitudes regarding sexuality, the laughter by Hurons when Father Le Caron tried to explain the Sixth Commandment regarding adultery. The Hurons simply stated, "It was impossible to keep that one."[13]

English colonists often called Native Americans "filthy." Originally, I was perplexed by this comment because of the English abhorrence of bathing in contrast to the daily plunge by most Indians into a river or other body of water. From the sixteenth to the nineteenth century, Europeans labeled Indians as "filthy" because of their seemingly unrepressed sexuality and not for their inattention to bathing.[14]

Another important cultural difference was in family organization. Most Native American tribes were organized into extended clans. Europeans wanted to replace the clan system with a nuclear family structure that would give power to the father. In the clan system, gender roles were divided by work. Women took care of domestic and agricultural work, and men did the hunting. The major responsibility for child rearing was not with the father, but with the mother and her relations within the clan.

Many European American men were offended by the power of women in the clan structure. On the other hand, James Axtell found that many colonial women captured by Indians preferred to remain with the tribe because of the higher status of women in Indian society in contrast with colonial society. Captured by Indians at the age of fifteen, Mary Jemison described female Indian work as being not so severe or hard as that done by white women. "In the summer season," she wrote, "we planted, tended and harvested our corn, and generally had all our children with us; *but had no master to oversee or drive us, so that we could work as leisurely as we pleased*." Axtell concludes, "Unless Jemison was correct, it would be virtually impossible to understand why so many women and girls chose to become Indians."[15]

Often, Native American women exercised political power. The Cherokees, in particular, were noted for having female leaders and frequently female warriors. White male settlers often spoke despairingly of the "petticoat" government of the Cherokees. Cherokee women decided the fate of captives, they made decisions in Women's Council that were relayed to the general tribe by the War Woman or Pretty Woman. Clan-mothers had the right to wage war. War Women, among the Cherokees, were called Beloved Women and had the power to free victims from the punishment prescribed by the general council.[16]

Paula Gunn Allen forcefully describes the consequences for Native American women and children of a nuclear family and authoritarian child-rearing practices. Allen describes these changes as "the replacing of a peaceful, nonpunitive, nonauthoritarian social system wherein women wield power by making social life easy and gentle with one based on child terrorization, male dominance, and submission of women to male authority."[17]

In summary, European American discussions of the education of Native Americans were focused on total cultural transformation. While many Native Americans wanted to become literate, white educators wanted religious and cultural conversion. For European American educators, the "civilizing" of Native Americans included the instilling of a work ethic; the creation of a desire to accumulate property; the repression of pleasure, particularly sexual pleasure, for work; the establishment of a nuclear family structure with the father in control; the reduction of the power of women; the implementation of authoritarian child-rearing practices; and the conversion to Christianity.

EARLY NATIVE AMERICAN EDUCATIONAL PROGRAMS

Contrary to the hopes of English colonists, Native Americans demonstrated little interest in being educated and converted by the colonists. And, contrary to many statements about "civilizing" and "saving" Native Americans, colonists put little effort or time into sharing their knowledge.

In the early seventeenth century, the meager efforts of the Virginia Company to educate Indians in colonial homes and to establish Henrico College for the education of Native Americans were doomed to failure because, as Margaret Szasz, writes, "the powerful Powhatan Algonquian saw their culture as superior to the colonial culture. As a result, Virginians encountered overwhelming difficulty in attempting to . . . educate their children. . . . "[18]

In the 1640s, criticism from England about the failure to convert Indians forced colonists into action. Leading these missionary efforts was John Eliot who is known as "the Apostle to the Indians." Eliot quickly discovered that Native Americans were not receptive to his preaching. Having learned to speak Native American languages, Eliot first preached on July 5, 1646 to a gathering of Indians at Dorchester Mill. Eliot's account of the experience is a clear indication of Native American attitudes towards colonial culture. "They gave no heed unto it," he recorded, "but were weary, and rather despised what I said."[19]

Setting the tone of religious intolerance that would characterize European American educational efforts into the twentieth century, the Massachusetts General Court declared in 1646, after Eliot's sermon, that any "Christian or pagan [obviously referring to Indians] . . . wittingly and willingly . . . deniing [sic] the true God, or his creation or government of the world . . . shalbe [sic] put to death." And, to assure compliance by Native Americans, the General Court enacted a law requiring that once a year Indians be informed of their possible execution for denying the validity on the Christian God.[20]

Eliot argued that Indians converted to Christianity should be separated from their villages and placed in small reservations called praying towns. Kept from contact with the "uncivilized" life of Native villages, praying Indians, according to Eliot, could become civilized. Eliot believed that helping praying Indians to live a true Christian life required punishment for such things as long hair and the killing of lice with teeth.[21]

The founding of Dartmouth College and the work of Eleazar Wheelock and Samson Occom represent the most famous colonial efforts at Native American education and the initiation of the tradition of using boarding schools to civilize Native Americans. Similar to later plans of the U.S. government, Wheelock advocated removing Indian children from contact with the tribal traditions of their families and placing them in boarding schools for cultural conversion. Also, similar to later arguments, Wheelock claimed that education was cheaper than war. Educate Native Americans to live like the colonists, Wheelock believed, and there would be no more Indian wars.

Wheelock's first educational success in the 1740s was Samson Occom, a Mohegan, who later went to England to raise money for the founding of Dartmouth. After that success, Wheelock established Moor's Charity School in 1754 which provided instruction in religion and classical training in Latin and Greek. Also, boys received instruction in farming and girls in household tasks. The vocational education was designed to prepare Native American students to live the farm life of a New Englander.[22]

With Wheelock's blessing, Samson Occom, went to England in 1766 where he successfully raised money for the founding of Dartmouth College. The Dartmouth charter reads, "for the education and instruction of youth of the Indian Tribes . . . and christianizing Children of Pagans . . . and also of English youth and others." Wheelock used the money to create a college that primarily served white youth.[23]

After the American Revolution, as I discuss in the next section, these rather faint-hearted efforts by colonists to "civilize" Native Americans were replaced by a major effort of the U.S. government to use deculturalization policies as a means of gaining Indian lands. In turn, Native Americans became aware that they would have to become literate if they were going to deal with this new government.

SCHOOLING AND THE COLONIZATION OF THE "FIVE CIVILIZED TRIBES"

A major problem facing the U.S. government after the Revolution was acquiring the lands of Native Americans to the south and west of the lands controlled by white settlers. Of particular concern were the tribes occupying southern lands in what is now North and South Carolina, Georgia, Florida, Alabama, Mississippi, and Tennessee. President George Washington and Secretary of War Henry Knox warned the Senate in 1789, "To conciliate the powerful tribes of Indians in the southern District [which included the Choctaw, Cherokee, Chickasaw, Creek, and Seminole tribes] amounting probably to fourteen thousand fighting Men, and to attach them firmly to the United States, may be regarded as highly worthy of the serious attention of government."[24]

Having fought a long and costly war with the British, the U.S. government did not have the resources to immediately embark upon a military campaign against the southern tribes. The easiest route to acquiring their lands was to purchase them through treaties. It is important to understand that the U.S. government treated the purchase of Native American lands as the same thing as bringing the land under the control of the laws of the American government. For instance, the traditional practice in Europe was that if an English person bought land in France, French laws continued to govern the land. In North America, Europeans assumed that the purchase of Native American lands resulted in governance by European American laws. For example, if traditional European practices were followed, Cherokee land purchased by the U.S. government would have remained under the governance of the Cherokee tribe rather than being placed under the control of U.S. laws.

Therefore, purchase was tantamount to conquest and it was cheaper than a military campaign. Washington proposed this approach in a 1783 letter to James Duane, who served as head of a select committee on Indian Affairs in the Continental Congress. Washington urged the purchase of Indian lands instead of expropriation. "In a word," Washington wrote, "there is nothing to be obtained by an Indian War but the Soil they live on and this can be had by purchase at less expense, and without bloodshed. . . . "[25] The famous Northwest Ordinance of 1787 held out the same promise of peace and negotiation for Indian lands. The Ordinance states: "The utmost good faith shall always be observed towards the Indians, their lands and property shall never be taken from them without their consent; and in their property, rights and liberty, they never shall be invaded or disturbed."[26]

U.S. government leaders decided that the best method of convincing the southern tribes to sell their lands was civilization programs. And, in what would later be used by Thomas Jefferson as a means of civilizing Native Americans, Washington proposed the establishment of official U.S. government trading houses on tribal lands as a means of "render[ing] tranquility with the savages permanent by creating ties of interest."[27]

When Thomas Jefferson became President in 1801, he also hoped trading houses would be the means for civilizing Native Americans and gaining their lands. The major flaw in these policies was the assumption that Indians would be willing to sell their lands. As Jefferson noted in a message to Congress in 1803, "the policy has long been gaining strength with them [Native Americans] of refusing absolutely all further sale on any conditions."[28] Faced with this resistance, Jefferson's problem was developing a plan that would cause tribes to sell their lands.

Jefferson was convinced that the cultural transformation of Native Americans was the key to acquiring tribal lands. For Jefferson, the solution to breaking down resistance to selling land involved transforming Native Americans into yeoman farmers who, living on farms and no longer dependent on hunting, would not need vast tracts of wilderness for hunting. In his first annual message to Congress in 1801, he informed the members that "efforts to introduce among them [Indians] the implements and practice of husbandry, and of the household arts" was successful. "They are becoming more and more sensible," he stated, "of the superiority of this dependence for clothing and subsistence over the precarious resources of hunting and fishing." He was pleased to report that as a result of learning European American methods of husbandry and agriculture, tribes "begin to experience an increase of population."[29]

As did many other European Americans, Jefferson believed it was important to teach Indians a desire for the accumulation of property and to extinguish the cultural practice of sharing. Similar to other arguments for the civilization of Native Americans, Jefferson linked the creation of the nuclear family with a desire to acquire property and the establishment of a formal government. Writing to the chiefs of the Cherokee Nation in 1806, he congratulated the tribe for beginning a transition from hunting to husbandry and farming. The nuclear family structure resulting from farming, he argued, would create a desire to accumulate and pass on property. "When a man has enclosed and improved his farm," Jefferson wrote, "builds a good house on it and raises plentiful stocks of animals, he will wish when he dies that *these things shall go to his wife and children, who he loves more than he does his other relations, and for whom he will work with pleasure during his life* (emphasis is mine)".[30]

The accumulation of property, Jefferson warned the Cherokees, requires the establishment of laws and courts. "When a man has property," Jefferson wrote, "earned by his own labor, he will not like to see another come and take it from him because he happens to be stronger, or else to defend it by spilling blood. You will find it necessary then to appoint good men, as judges, to decide rules you shall establish."[31]

By creating in Native Americans a desire for the accumulation of wealth and the purchase of manufactured goods on display at government trading houses, Jefferson believed, Indians would be willing to sell their lands to gain cash. In this manner, Native Americans would become part of a cash economy and would become dependent on manufactured goods.

In a special message to Congress urging the continuation of trading houses, Jefferson wrote that to counteract tribal resistance to selling land "and to provide an extension of territory which *the rapid increase of our numbers will call for* (emphasis is mine), two measures are deemed expedient." The first, he argued, was to encourage Indians to abandon hunting for agriculture and husbandry. "The extensive forests necessary in the hunting life," he told Congress, "will then become useless, and they will see advantage in exchanging them for the means of improving their farms and of increasing their domestic comfort." Second, he argued, the trading houses will make them aware of what they can purchase with the money earned from the sale of lands. Consequently, Jefferson asked Congress, "To multiply trading houses among them, and place within their reach those things *which will contribute more to their domestic comfort than the possession of extensive but uncultivated wilds* (emphasis is mine)."[32]

Jefferson wanted to change Native American values regarding the economy, government, family relations, and property, and manipulate desires regarding consumption of goods. Civilizing Native Americans, in this case, meant completely wedding them to an economy of increasing production and demand for new goods. "In leading them thus to agriculture, to manufactures, and civilization," Jefferson told Congress, "in bringing together their and our sentiments, and in preparing them ultimately to participate in the benefits of our Government, I trust and believe we are acting for their greatest good."[33]

U.S. government agents were the principle means for instituting Jefferson's civilization policies. Among the Cherokees, government agents were instructed to establish schools to teach women how to spin and sew and to teach men the use of farm implements and methods of husbandry. Agents acted as teachers and advertisers of manufactured goods. They were to begin the cultural transformation of Native Americans that would change Native American ideas about farming, families, government, and economic relations. At the end of his term, according to Francis Prucha, Jefferson felt vindicated by his policies of civilization. "The southern tribes, especially," Prucha writes, "were far ahead of the others in agriculture and the household arts and in proportion to this advancement identified their views with those of the United States."[34]

NOTES

1. Ronald Takaki, *A Different Mirror: A History of Multicultural America* (Boston: Little, Brown and Company, 1993), p. 28.
2. Ibid., pp. 28–29.
3. Dee Brown, *Bury My Heart at Wounded Knee: An Indian History of the American West* (New York: Henry Holt and Company, 1970), pp. 171–172.
4. Takaki, p. 79.
5. Takaki, pp. 79–80.
6. Takaki, p. 39.
7. See Harry Warfel, *Noah Webster: School Master to America* (New York: Macmillan, 1936).
8. Carl F. Kaestle, *Pillars of the Republic: Common Schools and American Society, 1780–1860* (New York: Hill and Wang, 1983), p. 103.
9. For a discussion of the attraction of Native American cultures to whites and the phenomenon of "white Indians," see James Axtell, *The Invasion Within: The Contest of Cultures in Colonial North America* (New York: Oxford University Press, 1985), pp. 302–327.
10. John Edwards, "The Choctaw Indians in the Middle of the Nineteenth Century," *Chronicles of Oklahoma* (1932):10, p. 410.
11. Quoted in George Pettit, *Primitive Education in North America* (Berkeley: University of California Press, 1936), p. 6.
12. Ibid., pp. 403–404.
13. Axtell, p. 123.
14. Francis Jennings, *The Invasion of America* (New York: W. W. Norton, 1975), pp. 49–50.
15. Axtell, p. 324.
16. Paula Gunn Allen, *The Sacred Hoop: Recovering the Feminine in American Indian Traditions* (Boston: Beacon Press, 1992), pp. 36–37.
17. Allen, pp. 40–41.
18. Margaret Szasz, *Indian Education in the American Colonies, 1607–1783* (Albuquerque: University of New Mexico Press, 1988), p. 259.
19. Ibid., p. 239.
20. Ibid., p. 241.
21. Ibid., pp. 249–251.
22. Ibid., pp. 191–258.
23. Jon Reyhner and Jeanne Eder, *A History of Indian Education* (Billings: Eastern Montana College, 1989), pp. 20–22.
24. Quoted in Francis Paul Prucha, *The Great Father: The United States Government and the American Indians* (Lincoln: University of Nebraska Press, 1984), p. 53.

25. "George Washington to James Duane. September 7, 1783." *Documents of United States Indian Policy, Second Edition*, edited by Francis Paul Prucha (Lincoln: University of Nebraska Press, 1990), pp. 1–2.
26. "Northwest Ordinance. July 13, 1787." Ibid., pp. 9–10.
27. "President Washington on Government Trading Houses. December 3, 1793." Ibid., p. 16.
28. "President Jefferson on Indian Trading Houses. 1803" Ibid., p. 21.
29. "First Annual Message. December 8, 1801," *The Life and Selected Writings of Thomas Jefferson* edited by Adrienne Koch and William Peden (New York: The Modern Library, 1944), p. 324.
30. "To the Chiefs of the Cherokee Nation. Washington, January 10, 1806." *The Life and Selected Writings of Thomas Jefferson*, p. 578.
31. Ibid., p. 579.
32. "President Jefferson on Indian Trading Houses. January 18, 1803," *Documents of United States Indian Policy*, pp. 21–22.
33. Ibid., p. 22.
34. Prucha, p. 143.

CHAPTER 2

Deculturalization and the Schooling of Native Americans

THOMAS L. McKENNEY: THE CULTURAL POWER OF SCHOOLING

Thomas McKenney's belief in the power of schooling to culturally transform Native Americans reflected the growing conviction among many European Americans that education was the key to social control and improvement of society. Born into a Quaker family on March 21, 1785, Thomas L. McKenney's religious values were reflected in policies stressing peace and Christianity during the fourteen years of his service as superintendent of Indian trade and, after the office was abolished in 1823, as head of the newly created Office of Indian Affairs from 1824 to 1830.[1]

A decade before the common-school movement, McKenney's ideas on the power of schooling were enacted by Congress in the Civilization Act of 1819. In the 1820s, McKenney advanced the argument that the creation of tribal school systems operated by white missionary teachers would culturally transform Native Americans in one generation. This extreme belief in the power of the school to change and control societies was later reflected in the thinking of common-school reformers in the 1830s and the rise of public schools.

Conceptualizing Indians as children, McKenney believed the key to civilizing them was schooling. Consequently, shortly after being appointed superintendent of Indian trade in 1816, McKenney's interests shifted from trade as a means of cultural transformation to the use of schools. By 1819, McKenney was able to convince Congress to pass the Civilization Fund Act to provide money for the support of schools among Indian tribes. Reflecting on his effort to gain approval of the legislation, McKenney wrote, "I did not doubt then, nor do I now, the capacity of the Indian for the highest attainments in civilization, in the arts and religion, but I was satisfied that no adequate plan had ever been adopted for this great reformation."[2]

Just prior to the adoption of the Civilization Fund Act, McKenney recounts, it appeared "to me to be propitious for the making of the experiment."[3] It is important to emphasize that McKenney considered the introduction of schools into Indian tribes as an "experiment" in what I call ideological management. Could schools "civilize" Native Americans? Could schools bring about a cultural transformation? At the time, McKenney didn't consider the possibility that some tribal members might resent and resist this attempt at cultural transformation. He believed that the time was right for the experiment because of relative peace with the tribes and, besides, "there were now several missionary stations already in operation, though on a small scale, all of them furnishing proof that a plan commensurate to the object, would reform and save, and bless this long neglected, and downtrodden people."[4]

The Civilization Fund Act of 1819 authorized the President to "employ capable persons of good moral character, to instruct them [Indians] in the mode of agriculture suited to their situation; and for teaching their children in reading, writing, and arithmetic." The legislation provided an annual sum of ten thousand dollars to be used by the President to fund the establishment of schools. The legislation specifically indicated that the funds were to be used with tribes "adjoining the frontier settlements of the United States." In practice, a large percentage of the money funded missionaries to set up schools among the Choctaws and Cherokees.[5]

By the late 1820s, McKenney was advocating a final solution to the problem of the southern tribes which involved their removal to lands west of the Mississippi for their protection and "civilization." After negotiating in 1827 with the Chickasaw Indians for their removal west of the Mississippi, McKenney wrote Secretary of War James Barbour that after removal the southern Indians should be guaranteed their lands in the west and "schools should be distributed over all their country. The children should be taken into these, and instructed . . . [in] reading, writing and arithmetic, in mechanics and the arts; and the girls in all the business of the domestic duties."[6]

Thinking of Indians as children, who only needed to be protected from evil and sent to school, he concluded that under the conditions of isolation and education Indians could be civilized in one generation. "Now can any one doubt," McKenney wrote, "that this system [schools in Indian Territory], would not lift them in a single generation to a level with ourselves?"[7]

THE MISSIONARY EDUCATORS

There was no objection to the U.S. government subsidizing Protestant missionary-educators under the provisions of the Civilization Act. From the perspective of the late twentieth century, government support of missionaries might be considered a violation of the First Amendment prohibition against government support of religion. But, for most European Americans in the early nineteenth century, public education and Protestantism went hand-in-hand. Throughout the nineteenth century, most educators did not think it was strange to begin the public school day with a prayer and a reading from a Protestant Bible. In fact, in the minds of most white Protestants in the early nineteenth century, it probably appeared logical and correct to use missionary-educators to "civilize" Native Americans, because "civilizing" included conversion to Christianity.

In the United States, Protestant churches organized to civilize Native Americans and to convert the entire non-Christian world. In the early nineteenth century, missionary-educators took the message of Protestantism to Asia, Africa, and the South Pacific. In 1810, the Presbyterian and Congregationalist churches founded the American Board of Commissioners for Foreign Missions (ABCFM). The ABCFM had a global mission and began sending missionaries abroad and to Native American tribes in 1812. In the minds of missionaries, Native Americans were foreign "heathen."[8]

Presbyterian missionaries sponsored by the ABCFM and later, the Board of Foreign Missionaries, believed that missionary work involved the manifest destiny of Anglo-Saxon culture to spread around the world. And, of course, the concept of manifest destiny included a belief that it was God's will that the U.S. government extend its power across the continent and over all Native American tribes. The Board of Foreign Missions believed it was proper for the U.S. Commissioner of Indian Affairs to aid missionary efforts, because they believed the spread of republican government to Indian nations required the spread of Protestantism and Anglo-Saxon culture.[9]

An example of combining civilization of Native Americas with the spread of Anglo-Saxon culture was Reverend James Ramsey's speech at a Choctaw school in 1846. Ramsey described his initial lecture to students and trustees in the following words: "I showed them [on a map] that the people who speak the English language, and who occupied so small a part of the world, and possessed the greatest part of its wisdom and knowledge; that knowledge they could thus see for themselves was power; and that power was to be obtained by Christianity alone."[10] Then he told them that the key to their success would be to continue the practice of establishing religious schools. In this way, they could share in the glory of Anglo-Saxon culture and Christianity.

The Presbyterian missionaries sent by the ABCFM had more influence on the leadership of Native American tribes than other missionary-educators. Presbyterians believed that conversion of the tribal leadership would result in Christianity and civilization trickling down to other tribal members. In contrast, Baptists and Methodists believed that their work should begin with conversion of the common full-blood Indian.[11]

All three religious denominations emphasized the importance of changing traditional customs of Native Americans while teaching reading and writing. For instance, the Presbyterian missionary Cyrus Kingsbury, called the "Apostle to the Choctaws," wrote

> It is our intention to embrace in their [Native American] education, that practical industry, and that literary, moral and religious instruction, which may qualify them for useful members of society; and for the exercise of those moral principles, and that genuine piety, which for the basis of true happiness.[12]

In the words of historian Michael Coleman, "These Presbyterians could accept nothing less than the total rejection of the tribal past, and the total transformation of each individual Indian, a cultural destruction and regeneration to be brought about by the Gospel of Jesus Christ."[13]

Similar to the Presbyterians, the Missionary Society of the Methodist Episcopal Church, the Kentucky Baptist Society for Propagating the Gospel among the Heathen, and other Protestant missionary organizations defined as their goal the replacement of Native American culture with the culture of white Anglo-Saxon Protestantism. While many Native Americans had simply asked for literacy, they received an education designed to bring about their cultural and religious conversion.

LANGUAGE AND NATIVE AMERICAN CULTURES

The relationship between language and culture is clearly evident in the differences between missionary efforts to develop written Native American languages and the creation of a written Cherokee language by Sequoyah. Missionaries wanted to develop written Native American languages so that they could translate religious tracts. Missionaries did not want to use a written Native American language as a means of preserving Native American history and religions. For missionaries, a written Native American language was another means of teaching Protestant Anglo-Saxon culture. Teaching of English was also considered another means of cultural transformation. Moravian educator John Gambold wrote, "It is indispensably necessary for their preservation that they should learn our *Language* and adopt our Laws and Holy Religion."[14]

In contrast, the development of a written Cherokee language by Sequoyah was for the purpose of preserving Cherokee culture. Missionaries reacted negatively to Sequoyah's invention because it threatened their efforts. Reverend Gambold wrote, regarding Sequoyah's invention, "The study of their language would in a great measure prove but time and labor lost. . . . it seems desirable that their Language, Customs, Manner of Thinking should be forgotten."[15]

In 1821 Sequoyah, a mixed-blood Cherokee whose English name was George Guess, returned to the Cherokee Nation from Arkansas with a Cherokee alphabet using 86 characters of his invention. Sequoyah was born in a small Cherokee village in Tennessee, served in the War of 1812, and joined a group of Cherokees in 1819 who immigrated to Arkansas. Sequoyah worked twelve years on the development of his alphabet. An important thing to note about Sequoyah's work is that he was illiterate and he did not speak English. Consequently, his approach to developing a written language was different from that of a literate missionary using English or another European language to render the Cherokee language into a written form. While he probably got the idea of having a written language from Europeans, Sequoyah's invention was based on his creation of characters to represent different sounds in the Cherokee language.[16]

The genius of Sequoyah's alphabet was that since each of the 86 characters matched a particular sound in the Cherokee language, it was possible for a Cherokee to quickly become literate in Cherokee. With diligence, a person speaking Cherokee could learn the alphabet in one day and learn to read Cherokee in one week. A Moravian missionary described the following changes resulting from Sequoyah's invention:

> The alphabet was soon recognized as an invaluable invention. . . . in little over a year, thousands of hitherto illiterate Cherokees were able to read and write their own language, teaching each other in cabins or by the roadside. The whole nation became an academy for the study of the system. Letters were written back and forth between the Cherokees in the east and those who had emigrated to the lands in Arkansas.[17]

The future editor of the first Native American newspaper, Elias Boudinot, recognized the importance of Sequoyah's invention and decided to publish a newspaper in English and Cherokee. While requesting funds in 1826 for his newspaper, Boudinot told the congregation at the First Presbyterian Church in Philadelphia that one of the most important things to happen to the tribe was the "invention of letters." He pleaded for funds for a printing press "with the types . . . to be composed of English letters and Cherokee characters. Those characters," he informed the congregation, "have now become extensively used in the nation; their religious songs are written in them; there is an astonishing eagerness in people of all classes and ages to acquire a knowledge of them. . . ."[18]

After his address in Philadelphia, Boudinot headed to Boston to collect the newly cast type in Sequoyah's symbols. He returned to the Cherokee Nation and on February 21, 1828 he published the first Native American newspaper, the *Cherokee Phoenix*, with columns written in English and Cherokee. Of primary importance for full-bloods, the newspaper published Cherokee laws in both English and Cherokee.

Despite the fact that missionaries had struggled for years to create a written Cherokee language, they were not very receptive to Sequoyah's invention. One important reason for their reluctance to embrace the new alphabet was that it required a knowledge of spoken Cherokee. None of the missionary educators had been able to learn Cherokee and, consequently, Sequoyah's symbols were of little use to them. In addition, many missionaries feared that if Cherokees learned to read and write in their own language, then they would never learn English. For most missionaries learning English was essential for the purpose of destroying traditional Cherokee culture. Therefore, while Sequoyah's invention proved a uniting force among full-blood Cherokees, it did not become a language of the missionary schools established on Cherokee lands in the east.

INDIAN REMOVAL AND CIVILIZATION PROGRAMS

By the time of Andrew Jackson's election to the presidency and his First Annual Message to Congress in December, 1829, he had concluded that civilization policies originating with Presidents Washington and Jefferson, and extended by the Civilization Act of 1819, had failed to educate southern tribes to the point where they would want to sell their lands. In fact, he worried that education was resulting in Indians gaining the tools to resist the policies of the U.S. government. Of course, gaining the ability to resist was precisely why the Cherokees had decided literacy was important.

In his First Annual Message to Congress, Jackson devoted considerable space to outlining his arguments for Indian removal to lands west of the Mississippi.[19]

One of the crucial parts of Jackson's argument was the right of white settlers to Indian lands. Previously, President Washington argued that Indian lands should be acquired by treaties and purchases. Now, President Jackson proposed a combination of treaties and exchange of lands for land west of the Mississippi. In addition, Jackson maintained that white settlers had rights to Indian lands that were not cultivated. In other words, he only recognized as legitimate claims by Indians for land on which they had made improvements. Claims could *not* be made for land, in Jackson's words, "on which they have neither dwelt nor made improvements, merely because they have seen them from the mountain or passed them in the chase."[20]

In proposing to set aside land west of the Mississippi for the relocation of Indians, Jackson promised to give each tribe control over the land and the right to establish any form of government. The only role of the United States government, Jackson argued, would be to preserve peace among the tribes and on the frontier. In this territory, Jackson declared, the "benevolent may endeavor to teach them the arts of civilization, and, by promoting union and harmony among them, to raise up an interesting commonwealth, destined to perpetuate the race and to attest the humanity and justice of this Government."[21] The key to fulfilling the humanitarian goals of removal would be education. In its final version, the Indian Removal Act of May 28, 1830 authorized the President to set aside lands west of the Mississippi for the exchange of Indian lands east of the Mississippi. In addition, the President was authorized to provide assistance to the tribes for their removal and resettlement on new lands.

In one of the most infamous acts in human history, entire nations of people were forced from their lands. Called the Trail of Tears, Indians died of cholera, exposure, contaminated food, and the hazards of frontier travel. Witnessing the removal of the Choctaws from Mississippi, missionary William Goode wrote, "Melancholy and dejected with their compulsory removal, years elapsed without much effort for improvement." He told the story of the drunken Choctaw who threw himself into the last boat leaving for Indian Territory shouting, "Farewell white man! Steal my Land!"[22] Near his home in 1832, Horatio Cushman recalls the sounds from the encampment of Choctaws waiting for removal: " . . . there came, borne upon the morn and evening breeze from every point of the vast encampment, faintly, yet distinctly, the plaintive sound of weeping."[23] After visiting the encampment, Cushman recorded this bleak portrait:

> The venerable old men . . . expressed the majesty of silent grief; yet there came now and then a sound that here and there swelled from a feeble moan to a deep, sustained groan—rising and falling till it died away just as it began . . . while the women and children,

> seated upon the ground, heads covered with shawls and blankets and bodies swinging forward and backward . . . sad tones of woe echoing far back from the surrounding but otherwise silent forests; while the young and middle-aged warriors, now subdued and standing around in silence profound, gazed into space . . . here and there was heard an inarticulate moan seeking expression in some snatch of song, which announced its leaving a broken heart.[24]

The Cherokees faced the horror of actual physical roundup by the U.S. Army. By 1838, only 2,000 of 17,000 Cherokees made the trip west. The remaining 15,000 did not seem to believe that they would be driven out of their country.[25]

In 1838, General Winfield Scott with a combined military force of 7,000 was placed in charge of the removal process. General Scott issued a proclamation that within a month every Cherokee man, woman, and child should be headed west. Scott's troops moved through the countryside surrounding houses, removing the occupants, looting and burning the houses, and forcing the families into stockades. Men and women were run down in the fields and forests as the troops viciously pursued their prey. Sometimes the troops found children at play by the side of the road and simple herded them into stockades without the knowledge of their parents. Besides stealing directly from the Cherokees, the troops and white outlaws drove off cattle and other livestock. The Cherokees placed in stockades were left destitute. A volunteer from Georgia, who later served as a colonel in the Confederate Army, said, "I fought through the Civil War and have seen men shot to pieces and slaughtered by thousands, but the Cherokee removal was the cruelest work I ever knew."[26]

The removal of tribes to Indian Territory raised the issue of the legal status of tribal governments and, as part of the operation of government, tribal school systems. This issue was clarified in a U.S. Supreme Court ruling in 1831 involving the extension of the laws of the state of Georgia over the Cherokee Nation. The Cherokees argued that this was illegal because they were a foreign nation. The question, as posed in the decision of the Court, was: "Is the Cherokee nation a foreign state in the sense in which that term is used in the Constitution?"[27] The Court argued that the section of the Constitution dealing with the regulation of commerce made a distinction between foreign nations, states, and Indian tribes. Consequently, Indian tribes are not foreign countries, but they are political entities that are distinct from states. In the words of the Court, Indian tribes are "domestic dependent nations. . . . they are in a state of pupilage. Their relation to the United States resembles that of a ward to his guardian."[28]

Once settled in Indian Territory, the tribes quickly engaged in the business of organizing governments and establishing school systems. Because of their segregation in Indian Territory, the tribal school systems were only for tribal children. In addition, in one of the many cultural and racial twists in history, since the tribes owned enslaved Africans, the tribes established segregated schools for freed Africans after the Civil War.

One example of a successful Native American school system was the one created by the Choctaws who sent their best graduates to the east to attend college. In 1842, the ruling council of the Choctaw Nation provided for the establishment of a comprehensive system of schools. A compulsory attendance law was enacted by the Choctaw Nation in 1889.

The Choctaw schools were developed in cooperation with the missionaries. In this regard, Superintendent of Indian Affairs Thomas McKenney's dream of establishing schools in Indian Territory became a reality. The Spencer Academy (the author's uncle, Pat Spring, died in the fire that burned down the academy in 1896) was opened in 1844 and the Armstrong Academy in 1846. By 1848, the Choctaws had nine boarding schools paid for by tribal funds. In addition, a system of day or neighborhood schools was organized, and by 1860 these schools enrolled 500 students. After the Civil War, the Choctaws established a system of segregated schools for the children of freed slaves.[29]

In addition, an adult literacy program was developed by missionaries through a system of Saturday and Sunday schools. Whole families would camp near a school or church to receive instruction in arithmetic, reading, and writing. Instruction was bilingual in both Choctaw and English. While there were not many texts in Choctaw, missionaries did translate many portions of the Bible, hymn books, moral lectures, and other religious tracts into Choctaw.[30]

Many teachers were Choctaws educated in tribal schools. The teachers were examined in the common-school subjects and the

Choctaw constitution. Teachers followed a course of study modeled on that of neighboring states and taught in English, using the *Choctaw Definer* to help children translate from Choctaw into English.

The Spencer Academy for boys and the New Hope Academy for girls were the leading schools. The children who attended these schools were selected by district trustees until 1890 and after that by county judges. Selection was based on "promptness in attendance and their capacity to learn fast."[31] Only one student could be selected from any particular family.

In 1885, the tribal council removed the two academies from missionary management and placed them under the control of a board of trustees. In 1890, a school law was enacted that required male teachers at the Spencer Academy to be college graduates and to have the ability to teach Greek, Latin, French, and German, and female teachers at the New Hope Academy to have graduated from a college or normal school and to be able to teach two modern languages besides English. The faculty of both schools included both white and Choctaw instructors.

The success of the Choctaw educational system was paralleled by that of the Cherokee Nation. The Cherokees were given land just north of the Choctaw Nation. In 1841, after removal, the Cherokee National Council organized a national system of schools with eleven schools in eight districts, and in 1851 it opened academies for males and females. By the 1850s, the majority of teachers in these schools were Cherokee. Jon Reyhner and Jeanne Eder write, "By 1852 the Cherokee Nation had a better common school system than the neighboring states of Arkansas and Missouri."[32]

The success of the Choctaw and Cherokee school systems was highlighted in a congressional report released in 1969. The report noted that "In the 1800s, for example, the Choctaw Indians of Mississippi and Oklahoma [Indian Territory] operated about 200 schools and academies and sent numerous graduates to eastern colleges."[33] The report went on to praise the Cherokee schools. In the words of the report, "Using bilingual teachers and Cherokee texts, the Cherokees, during the same period, controlled a school system which produced a tribe almost *100% literate* [emphasis is mine]."[34] The report concluded, "Anthropologists have determined that as a result of this school system, the literacy level in English of western

Oklahoma Cherokees was higher than the white populations of either Texas or Arkansas."[35]

NATIVE AMERICANS: RESERVATIONS AND BOARDING SCHOOLS*

As white settlers moved into western lands in the latter part of the nineteenth century, leaders in the U.S. government were forced to reconsider their relationships to tribes and their attempts to "civilize" Indians. First, there was the problem of land on which to settle displaced tribes. Unlike in the 1820s and 1830s, there was a realization that white settlement would eventually cover most of the continent. In 1858, Commissioner of Indian Affairs Charles E. Mix, in his annual report, declared that the U.S. government had made several serious errors in dealing with the southeastern tribes, including "the assignment to them of too great an extent of country, to be held in common."[36] Holding large tracts of land in common, according to Commissioner Mix, limited the attempts to civilize the Indian because it prevented Indians from learning the value of separate and independent property.

Reservations and allotment programs were the responses to the land issue. The reservation system combined with education was considered by the U.S. government as the best method of dealing with what Commissioner of Indian Affairs Luke Lea called the "wilder tribes."[37] In the *Annual Report of the Commissioner of Indian Affairs* in 1850, Commissioner Lea argued that certain Indian tribes, specifically the Sioux and Chippewas, had an "insatiable passion for war" and that it was "necessary that they be placed in positions where they can be controlled."[38] Once concentrated in reservations where they could be controlled, the tribes would be compelled to remain until they proved themselves to be civilized. Under this system, the federal government was to supply agricultural implements to aid in this process of civilization.

Provisions for manual labor schools on reservations were specified in Commissioner Mix's report of 1858. Mix argued that reserva-

* I would like to thank the librarians and staff at the Huntington Free Library of the National Museum of the American Indian for their help in finding material on the education of Native Americans.

tion sites should be selected that would minimize contact with whites and provide opportunities for Indians to learn agricultural skills. To aid in the process of preparing Indians for agriculture, manual labor schools were to be established that would teach basic skills in reading, writing, arithmetic, and agricultural skills. Of particular importance, according to Commissioner Mix, was the role of manual labor schools in molding the character of future generations of Indians in what he called "habits of industry." To carry out this enterprise, Commissioner Mix recommended that a military force should remain in the vicinity of the reservations "to aid in controlling the Indians."[39]

Adding to the problem for government officials, western Indians displayed a great deal more resistance to white incursions onto their lands. This resulted in Indian wars across the plains of the West during the latter half of the nineteenth century. In 1867, Congress created an Indian Peace Commission to deal with the warring tribes. The Indian Peace Commission advocated different methods for the education and civilization of Indians. The Peace Commission placed emphasis on the role of education in converting Indians to civilization. Nathaniel Taylor, Chairman of the Peace Commission, told Crow Indians at Fort Laramie: "Upon the reservations you select, we . . . will send you teachers for your children."[40] According the Jon Reyhner and Jeanne Eder, this promise was embodied in the Treaty of Fort Laramie with the Sioux and their allies.[41]

The members of the Peace Commission were not entirely satisfied with the traditional attempts to educate Indians, particularly with regard to language. The Indian Peace Commission report of 1868 states that differences in language were a major source of the continuing friction between whites and Indians. Therefore, according to the report, an emphasis on the teaching of English would be a major step in reducing hostilities and civilizing Native Americans. In the words of the report: "Through sameness of language is produced sameness of sentiment and thought; customs and habits are moulded [sic] and assimilated in the same way, and thus in process of time the differences producing trouble would have been gradually obliterated."[42]

Replacing the use of native languages with English, destroying Indian customs, and teaching allegiance to the U.S. government became the major educational policies of the U.S. government toward

Indians during the latter part of the nineteenth century. An important part of these educational policies was the boarding school, which was designed to remove children from their families at an early age and thereby isolate them from the language and customs of their parents and tribes. These boarding schools were quite different from those operated by the Choctaws in Indian Territory, which were somewhat elite institutions within their educational system and were not designed to destroy Indian customs and languages.

In *A History of Indian Education*, Jon Reyhner and Jeanne Eder demonstrate the connections between the establishment of boarding schools for Indians and the history of black education in the South. The first off-reservation boarding school was the Carlisle Indian School, established in Carlisle, Pennsylvania, in 1879. The founder of the school, Richard Pratt, had commanded an African-American cavalry in Indian Territory between 1867 and 1875. According to Reyhner and Eder, Pratt's interest in founding a boarding school was sparked when he took seventeen adult Indian prisoners of war to Hampton Institute.[43] Hampton Institute played a major role in the development of African-American education in the South. Booker T. Washington was educated at Hampton and used it as a model when he established Tuskegee Normal and Industrial Institute in 1881. The primary purpose of Hampton was to prepare freed slaves to be teachers who could instill work values in other freed slaves. In the words of historian James Anderson, "The primary aim [of Hampton] was to work the prospective teachers long and hard so that they would embody, accept, and preach an ethic of hard toil or the 'dignity of labor.' "[44]

Pratt not only wanted to instill the work ethic in Indian children but also, as he told a Baptist group, immerse "Indians in our civilization and when we get them under [hold] them there until they are thoroughly soaked."[45] The slogan for the Carlisle Indian School reflected the emphasis on changing the cultural patterns of Indians: "To civilize the Indian, get him into civilization. To keep him civilized, let him stay."[46]

Pratt's educational philosophy embodied the principles behind the allotment movement of the latter part of the nineteenth century. The allotment program, which was applied to the Five Civilized Tribes with the breakup of Indian Territory, was designed to distribute commonly held tribal property to individual Indians. It was assumed that individual ownership would instill the capitalistic values of white civilization in Indians. In fact, tribal ownership was viewed as a form of socialism that was antithetical to the values of white American society. Also, the allotment program was another method of dealing with the Indian land problem. In the *Annual Report of the Commissioner of Indian Affairs* in 1881, Commissioner of Indian Affairs Hiram Price criticized previous attempts to civilize Indians because they did not teach the necessity of labor. This could be accomplished, Price argued, only when individual Indians were made responsible for their own economic welfare. This could be done, he contended, by allotting Indians "a certain number of acres of land which they may call their own."[47]

Pratt attacked the tribal way of life as socialistic and contrary to the values of "civilization." Reflecting the values of economic individualism, Pratt complained about missionary groups who did not "advocate the disintegration of the tribes and the giving to individual Indians rights and opportunities among civilized people."[48] He wrote to the Commissioner of Indian Affairs in 1890, "Pandering to the tribe and its socialism as most of our Government and mission plans do is the principal reason why the Indians have not advanced more and are not advancing as rapidly as they ought."[49]

Between the founding of the Carlisle Indian School in 1879 and 1905, twenty-five nonreservation boarding schools were opened throughout the country.[50] It is important to emphasize the *nonreservation* location of the boarding schools because of the educational philosophy that Indian children should be removed from family and tribal influences.

An important issue for both nonreservation boarding schools and schools on reservations was the teaching of English. As discussed previously, the attitude of many white educators in the latter part of the nineteenth century was that elimination of tribal languages and the learning of English would lead to the absorption and practice of white values by Indians. In the *Annual Report of the Commissioner of Indian Affairs* in 1887, Commissioner J. D. C. Adkins ordered the exclusive use of English at all Indian schools. Atkins pointed out that this policy was consistent with the requirement that only English be taught in public schools in territories acquired by the United States from Mexico, Spain, and Russia. Comparing the conquest of Indians to the German occupation of the French provinces of Alsace and Lorraine, where it was required that German rather than French be used in the schools, Atkins declared, "No unity or community of feeling can be established among different peoples unless they are brought to speak the same languages, and thus become imbued with like ideas of duty."[51]

Also, in an attempt to build a sense of community with the white population, it was hoped that Indian children would transfer their allegiance from their tribal governments to the federal government. Consequently, in 1889, Commissioner of Indian Affairs Thomas J. Morgan issued "Instructions to Indian Agents in Regard to Inculcation of Patriotism in Indian Schools," which required that an American flag be flown in front of every Indian school. The instructions state, "the 'Stars and Stripes' should be a familiar object, and students should be taught to reverence the flag as a symbol of their nation's power and protection."[52] In addition, the instructions required the teaching of American history and the principles of the U.S. government. There was no suggestion in the instructions that the history of Native Americans and their governments be taught in the schools. Also, the instructions called for the teaching of patriotic songs and the public recitation of "patriotic selections."[53]

In one of the more interesting uses of celebrating national holidays as a method of building support for government policies, Commissioner Morgan's instructions required that schools inculcate in students allegiance to government policies designed to break up tribal lands. After a sentence requiring the celebration of Washington's birthday, Decoration Day, the Fourth of July, Thanksgiving, and Christmas, the instructions state: "It will also be well to observe the anniversary of the day upon which the 'Dawes bill' for giving to Indians allotments of land in severalty become a law, viz, February 8, 1887, and to use that occasion to impress upon Indian youth the enlarged scope and opportunity given them by this law and the new obligations which it imposes."[54]

In 1889, Commissioner Morgan wrote a bulletin on "Indian Education" that outlined the goals and policies of Indian schools. The bulletin was distributed by the U.S. Bureau of Education with an introduction written by the Commissioner of Education, William T. Harris. In the introduction, Harris praised what he called "the new education for our American Indians," particularly the effort "to obtain control of the Indian at an early age, and to seclude him as much as possible from the tribal influences."[55] Harris singled out the boarding school as an important step in changing the character of American Indians. Harris argued that it was necessary to save the American Indian, but, he wrote, "We cannot save him and his patriarchal or tribal institution both together. To save him we must take him up into our civilization."[56]

Commissioner Morgan opened the bulletin with a statement of general principles of education for what he identified as a Native American population of 250,000 with a school population of 50,000. These general principles called for systematizing the system of Indian education, increasing its availability to Indian children, and making it compulsory for all Native American children to attend school. In addition, Indian education was to place special stress on vocational training for jobs and on teaching English. With regard to instruction in English, the bulletin states, "Only English should be allowed to be spoken, and only English-speaking teachers should be employed in schools supported wholly or in part by the Government."[57] Also, the general principles stressed the importance of teaching allegiance to the U.S. government. As an added note, Morgan stressed the importance of bringing together the members of many different tribes in boarding schools as a means of reducing antagonisms between them.

After outlining the general principles of Indian education, Morgan turned to the issue of the high school. Morgan noted that the government at that time was not supporting high schools for American Indians but only nonreservation boarding schools, reservation boarding schools, and day schools. Morgan favored the introduction of high schools for Indians as a means of breaking "the shackles of . . . tribal provincialism."[58] In advocating high schools, Morgan stressed the character-training qualities of a secondary education. He states, "The whole course of training [high school] should be fairly saturated with moral ideas, fear of God, and respect for the rights of others; love of truth and fidelity to duty; personal purity, philanthropy, and patriotism."[59]

Similar to the goals he gave for a high school education, he argued that grammar schools should stress systematic habits, "fervent patriotism," and the duties of citizens. Morgan stressed the character-training aspects of grammar schools, which he felt should develop an independent economic person as compared to an Indian who is dependent on communal tribal living. Reflecting the reality of how Indian schools were conducted, Morgan states that in grammar school: "No pains should be spared to teach them that their future must depend chiefly upon their own exertions, character, and endeavors. . . . In the sweat of their faces must they eat bread."[60]

Morgan also advocated early childhood education as a method of counteracting the influence of the Indian home. Similar to the boarding school, early childhood education would help to strip away the influences of Indian culture and language. Morgan states, "Children should be taken at as early an age as possible, before camp life has made an indelible stamp upon them."[61]

With hindsight, one might consider this plan of Indian education as one of the great endeavors to destroy cultures and languages and replace them with another culture and language. The key to the process was the removal of children from the influences of family and tribe and their placement in educational institutions where they would not be allowed to speak their native languages or practice native customs. As part of this educational effort, there was a concerted effort through a forced program of patriotism to have Indians switch their loyalties from their tribal governments to the federal government.[†]

The conditions in boarding schools lived up to Morgan's previously quoted edict: "In the sweat of their faces must they eat bread." During the 1920s, a variety of investigators of Indian schools were horrified by the conditions they found. At the Rice Boarding School in Arizona, Red Cross investigators found that children were fed "bread, black coffee, and syrup for breakfast; bread and boiled potatoes for dinner; more bread and boiled potatoes for supper."[62] In addition to a poor diet, overcrowded conditions contributed to the spread of tuberculosis and trachoma.

Using a paramilitary form of organization, boarding schools were supported by the labor of the students. As early as the fifth grade, boys and girls attended classes for half the day and worked

[†] The emphasis on patriotism is also reflected in the fact that the first rule of Indian school service was: "1. There shall be a flagstaff at each school, and in suitable weather the flag of the United States shall be hoisted each morning and taken down at sunset." Department of the Interior, United States Indian Service, *Rules for the Indian School Service 1913* (Washington, D.C.: U.S. Government Printing Office, 1913), p. 3.

for the other half. As part of the plan to teach agricultural methods, children raised crops and tended farm animals. The paramilitary organization was reflected in the constant drilling of students. The children were given little time for recreation. They were awakened at 5 A.M. and marched to the dining room, then marched back to the dormitories and classrooms. At the Albuquerque Indian School, students marched in uniforms with dummy rifles. For punishment children were flogged with ropes, and some boarding schools contained their own jails. In the 1920s, anthropologist Oliver La Farge called the Indian schools "penal institutions—where little children were sentenced to hard labor for a term of years to expiate the crime of being born of their mothers."[63]

THE "MERIAM REPORT"

The publication of the *Meriam Report* in 1928 began the process that ended this massive educational effort to change the language and culture of an entire people. The report was based on investigations conducted in 1926 by the Institute for Government Research at Johns Hopkins University at the request of the Secretary of Interior, Hubert Work. The report was known by the name of the principal investigator, Louis Meriam, and it was published as *The Problem of Indian Administration.*[64]

The report stated that the most fundamental need in Indian education was a change in government attitude. The report accurately stated that education in "the past has proceeded largely on the theory that it is necessary to remove the Indian child as far as possible from his home environment."[65] Completely reversing this educational philosophy, the report stated that "the modern point of view in education and social work lays stress on upbringing in the natural setting of home and family life."[66]

The report went on to argue that the routine and discipline of Indian schools destroyed initiative and independence. In addition, the report criticized the provision of only half a day of schooling and of working students at heavy labor at a young age. In particular, the report was critical of boarding schools and the isolation of children from their families and communities.[67]

Ironically—at least from the standpoint of the previous history of Indian education—federal policy after the issuance of the *Meriam*

Report stressed community day schools and the support of native cultures. The report argued that community day schools would serve the purpose of integrating education with reservation life. During the 1930s, Indian education placed stress on community schools and the rebuilding of the cultural life of American Indians. As I will discuss in a later chapter, these policies changed dramatically in the 1950s and 1960s with attempts to terminate tribes and with Indian participation in the civil rights movement.[68] In the end, the legacy of the allotment program and the educational efforts of the latter part of the nineteenth century was increasing illiteracy among the Five Civilized Tribes of the Indian Territory and the destruction of family life and Indian customs on the reservations. For the rest of the century, American Indians would attempt to rebuild what the federal government had destroyed.

NOTES

1. Herman J. Viola, "Introduction," *Thomas L. McKenney: Memoirs, Official and Personal*, edited by Herman J. Viola (Lincoln: University of Nebraska Press, 1973), pp. vii–xxvii.
2. Viola, p. 34.
3. Ibid., p. 34.
4. Ibid., p. 35.
5. "Civilization Fund Act. March 3, 1819." *Documents of United States Indian Policy, Second Edition*, edited by Francis Paul Prucha (Lincoln: University of Nebraska Press, 1990), p. 33.
6. "Thomas L. McKenney to Department of War, May 1, 1829," in *Thomas L. McKenney: Memoirs, Official and Personal*, edited by Herman J. Viola (Lincoln: University of Nebraska Press, 1973), p. 335.
7. Ibid., p. 18.
8. See Michael C. Coleman, *Presbyterian Attitudes toward American Indians, 1837–1893* (Jackson: University of Mississippi Press, 1985).
9. Coleman, pp. 38–42.
10. Ibid., p. 42.
11. William G. McLoughlin, *Cherokees and Missionaries 1789–1839* (New Haven: Yale University Press, 1984), pp. 135–151.
12. Quoted in Horatio Bardwell Cushman, *History of the Choctaw, Chickasaw, and Natchez Indians*, edited by Angie Debo (New York: Russell & Russell, 1972), p. 99. Cushman's book, originally published in 1899, is an important primary source on the history and cultural traditions of the Choctaws in the nineteenth century. Cushman was born at the

Mayhew missionary station in the Choctaw Nation where his parents were sent in 1820 by the American Board of Commissioner for Foreign Missions. Cushman's book is full of fond memories of growing up at Mayhew and participating in Choctaw life. He personally knew the Folsom, Pitchlynn, and Leflore families. See Angie Debo's foreword to the book.

13. Coleman, pp. 5–6.
14. William G. McLoughlin, *Cherokee Renascence in the New Republic*, (Princeton: Princeton University Press, 1986), pp. 354.
15. McLoughlin, *Cherokee Renascence in the New Republic*, pp. 354.
16. See Grant Foreman, *Sequoyah* (Norman: University of Oklahoma Press, 1938).
17. Ibid., p. 11.
18. Speech is reprinted in Ralph Henry Gabriel, *Elias Boudinot, Cherokee & His America* (Norman: University of Oklahoma Press, 1941), pp. 108–109.
19. "President Jackson on Indian Removal. December 8, 1829." Prucha, *Documents of*, pp. 47–48.
20. Ibid., p. 48.
21. "President Jackson," in Prucha, *Documents of*, p. 48.
22. William H. Goode, *Outposts of Zion, With Limnings of Mission Life* (Cincinnati: Poe & Hitchcock, 1864), p. 194.
23. Cushman, p. 114.
24. Ibid., p. 115.
25. See Foreman, pp. 251–315, for an account of the removal process.
26. Quoted by Foreman, p. 287.
27. "Cherokee Nation v. Georgia 1831," in Prucha, *Documents of*, p. 58.
28. Ibid., p. 59.
29. Quoted in Angie Debo, *The Rise and Fall of the Choctaw Republic* (Norman: University of Oklahoma Press, 1961), p. 180.
30. Ibid., p. 62.
31. Ibid., p. 238.
32. Jon Reyhner and Jeanne Eder, *A History of Indian Education* (Billings: Eastern Montana College, 1989), p. 34.
33. *Indian Education: A National Tragedy—A National Challenge 1969*, Report of the Committee on Labor and Public Welfare, U.S. Senate, 91st Congress, 1st Session (Washington, D.C.: U.S. Government Printing Office, 1969), p. 25.
34. Ibid.
35. Ibid.
36. "Indian Commissioner Mix on Reservation Policy," in Prucha, p. 92.
37. "Indian Commissioner Lea on Reservation Policy," in Ibid., p. 82.
38. Ibid.
39. "Indian Commissioner Mix," in Prucha, *Documents of*, p. 95.

40. Reyhner and Eder, p. 38.
41. Ibid., p. 39.
42. "Report of the Indian Peace Commission. January 7, 1868," in Prucha, *Documents of*, p. 107.
43. Reyhner and Eder, pp. 79–80.
44. James D. Anderson, *The Education of Blacks in the South 1860–1935* (Chapel Hill: University of North Carolina Press, 1988), p. 34.
45. Quoted in Reyhner and Eder, p. 80.
46. Ibid.
47. "Indian Commissioner Price on Civilizing Indians. October 24, 1881," in Prucha, *Documents of*, p. 155.
48. Quoted in Reyhner and Eder, p. 81.
49. Ibid.
50. Ibid., p. 86.
51. "Use of English in the Indian Schools. September 21, 1887," in Prucha, *Documents of*, p. 175.
52. "Inculcation of Patriotism in Indian Schools. December 10, 1889," in Prucha, *Documents of*, p. 181.
53. Ibid., pp. 180–181.
54. Ibid., p. 181.
55. General T. J. Morgan, "Indian Education," Bureau of Education, Bulletin No. 1, 1889 (Washington, D.C.: U.S. Government Printing Office, 1890), p. 4.
56. Ibid., p. 5.
57. Ibid., p. 9.
58. Ibid., p. 12.
59. Ibid.
60. Ibid., p. 16.
61. Ibid., p. 17.
62. Margaret Szasz, *Education and the American Indian: The Road to Self-Determination, 1928–1973* (Albuquerque: University of New Mexico Press, 1974), p. 19.
63. Quoted in Ibid., p. 22.
64. Lewis Meriam, *The Problem of Indian Administration* (Baltimore: The Johns Hopkins Press, 1928).
65. Ibid., p. 346.
66. Ibid.
67. Ibid., pp. 346–403.
68. See Szasz, *Education and the American Indian*, pp. 37–106; and Reyhner and Eder, *History of Indian Education*, pp. 102–109.

CHAPTER 3

Deculturalization of Puerto Ricans

Educational policy regarding Puerto Rico followed a pattern similar to that for Native Americans. The policy was based on a desire to win the loyalty of a conquered people and stabilize control of Puerto Rico as part of a broader strategy for maintaining U.S. influence in the Caribbean and Central America. Puerto Rico; Guantanamo Bay, Cuba; and the Panama Canal Zone were the linchpins of this strategy.[1] The use of education as part of the colonization of Puerto Rico was explicitly stated in 1902 in the annual report of the second commissioner of education, Samuel Lindsay: "Colonization carried forward by the armies of war is vastly more costly than that carried forward by the armies of peace, whose outpost and garrisons are the public schools of the advancing nation."[2]

Consequently, U.S. educational policy in Puerto Rico emphasized building loyalty to the U.S. flag and institutions, as well as deculturalization. The patriotic emphasis was similar to the Americanization programs directed at Native Americans. And, just as U.S. and state educational policies attempted to strip Indians of their languages and cultures, U.S. educational policy in Puerto Rico attempted to replace Spanish with English as the majority language and introduce children to the dominant U.S. culture.

Puerto Rico became a colony of the United States in 1898 at the conclusion of the Spanish-American War. The war represented the final demise of Spanish empire in the Americas. The events leading up to the Spanish-American War were primarily centered in Cuba where, prior to the outbreak of the war, a liberation army composed of Cuban rebels revolted against Spanish rule and economic domination by foreign sugar and tobacco industries. The liberation army marched through the countryside torching plantations and plunging Cuba into economic chaos. The Spanish response was brutal: 200,000 Spanish troops were sent to Cuba to stop the liberation army, and the infamous concentration camp order was issued. The concentration camp order moved women, children, and men from villages into garrison towns as a method of cutting off all support to the rebel army. Citizens were executed or their property confiscated if they were found traveling outside garrison towns without a passport.

The U.S. government was interested in the rebellion from several perspectives. First, there was an interest in reducing Spanish influence in the Americas. Within this context, the government was sympathetic to the liberation army's goal of ousting the Spanish. Second, the government was interested in protecting American-owned sugar and tobacco plantations. This meant economic stabilization. For this purpose, the U.S. government wanted the establishment of a stable democratic government that would protect the property interests of foreign investors. As a result of this concern, the U.S. government was not interested in the liberation army ruling Cuba at the conclusion of the war. Third, the U.S. government was interested in establishing military bases in the Caribbean. But, because of the politics surrounding the U.S. entry into the war, Puerto Rico became a colony of the United States rather than Cuba. Consequently, for military purposes, Guantanamo Bay, Cuba, was retained by the United States and military bases were established in Puerto Rico.

The event that sparked a congressional declaration of war was the sinking of the battleship *Maine* in Havana harbor on February 15, 1898. The immediate reaction was to claim that the sinking had been caused by the Spanish, but a later investigation found that a coal fire on the ship had caused a powder magazine to explode. Even though the Spanish might not have been responsible for the sinking, "Remember the *Maine*" became the rallying call for the war.

As a result of the rebel war and the sinking of the *Maine*, President William McKinley asked Congress for a joint resolution authorizing intervention in Cuba. The resolution passed by Congress called on the Spanish to abandon all claims to governing Cuba and to remove all its forces from the island. An important part of the resolution stated that the United States had no intention of exercising sovereignty over Cuba.

Spain, of course, considered the resolution a declaration of war. And the war quickly escalated to global proportions. On one side of the world, the U.S. Navy sailed into Manila in the Philippines. On the other side of the world, American troops joined the Liberation Army to oust the Spanish from Cuba. On October 18, 1898, U.S. forces, which had invaded Puerto Rico less than three months previously, raised the U.S. flag in San Juan and declared the end of Spanish rule and the beginning of U.S. dominion.

While events in Cuba were the main cause for the United States initiating the conflict, the final treaty focused on other Spanish territorial possessions. The U.S. Congress had already declared its intention not to rule Cuba; consequently, the United States demanded that Spain secede Puerto Rico, the island of Guam in the Central Pacific, and the Philippines. With the signing of the treaty on December 10, 1898, the U.S. military gained strategic bases in the Caribbean, the Pacific, and the Far East. In 1901, before relinquishing Cuba, the U.S. Congress passed legislation dictating that Cuba sell or lease lands for naval stations to the United States. This paved the way for the United States to establish a naval base at Guantanamo Bay, Cuba.[3]

THE AMERICANIZATION OF PUERTO RICO

When considering U.S. educational policy in Puerto Rico, it is important to understand that the citizens of Puerto Rico did not ask to become part of the United States. In fact, the goal of the independence movement in Puerto Rico throughout the nineteenth century was independence from Spain, not cession to the United States. Similar to its actions in Cuba, Spain attempted to crush any attempts to gain liberation from its rule. Typical of the independence movement was the Puerto Rican Revolutionary Committee, which, in 1863, marched under the banner "Liberty or Death. Long Live Free Puerto Rico."

In addition, in 1897, the year before the outbreak of the Spanish-American War, Spain declared Puerto Rico an autonomous state. The residents of the now former colony of Spain quickly established a constitutional republican form of government; however, Spain still appointed the governor, who had restricted power. The newly independent government assumed power in July 1898, just before the landing of U.S. troops.

Therefore, after a long struggle for an independence that was quickly snatched away by an invading U.S. military, Puerto Rican citizens did not welcome subjugation by the U.S. government. In fact, Puerto Rican resistance to U.S. control, while not so strong as it was in the early twentieth century, continues to this day.

The anger among Puerto Ricans was heightened by the fact that the United States immediately placed them under the control of a military government operated by the War Department. Within less than a year, Puerto Rico went from being an autonomous state to being ruled by a military dictatorship.

The strong Puerto Rican independence movement contributed to a wave of resistance to the educational policies designed for Americanization and deculturalization. A list of these policies was compiled by Aida Negron De Montilla in her book *Americanization in Puerto Rico and the Public-School System 1900–1930*. I provide here a summary of the list followed by an explanation of how these policies evolved.

In examining this list, you should consider the items in the broad context of how a nation can use schools to impose its will on a conquered people. This is a case study in both an attempt to dominate through education and resistance to that domination. Some of the items in the list are presented as "attempts" because of the high level of resistance to these plans by the Puerto Rican people.

Summary List of Americanization Policies in Public Schools in Puerto Rico

1. Required celebration of U.S. patriotic holidays, such as the Fourth of July, which had not been celebrated prior to conquest.
2. Patriotic exercises designed to create allegiance to the United States, such as pledging allegiance to the U.S. flag and studying important historical figures of U.S. history.
3. Replacing local textbooks and curricula with ones reflecting the way of life in the United States.
4. Attempts to expel teachers and students who engaged in anti-United States activities.
5. Attempts to use teachers from the United States as opposed to local teachers.
6. Introduction of organizations, such as the Boy Scouts of America, to promote allegiance to the United States.
7. Attempts to replace Spanish with English as the language of instruction.[4]

The first U.S. commissioner of education in Puerto Rico, Martin Grove Brumbaugh, captured the general thrust of these policies when he wrote in a preface to a history book, "President McKinley declared to the writer that it was his desire 'to put the conscience of the American people in the islands of the sea.' "[5] Brumbaugh was appointed in 1900, when military rule was replaced with a colonial government established by Congress under the Foraker Act. With the passage of the Foraker Act, which was in effect between 1900 and 1917, the President was given the power to appoint a commissioner of education for Puerto Rico.

While the military was in control, the educational system was organized along the lines of a U.S. model. In addition, the War Department created a commission to recommend educational policies for the island. The commission's report became a guide for Brumbaugh and the next six commissioners of education. The report outlined the basic methods of Americanization. It recommended that Puerto Rico have "the same system of education and the same character of books" as the United States, that teachers be "Americans," and that students be instructed in the English language.[6]

The commission's attitude about the power of education was similar to those who believed that Native Americans could be Americanized in one generation. At times, the language of the report gives the school an almost mystical power. "Put an American schoolhouse in every valley and upon every hilltop in Porto [sic] Rico," the report states, "and in these places . . . American schoolteachers, and the cloud of ignorance will disappear as the fog flies before the morning sun."[7]

While the report stressed Americanization, it cannot be considered simply a cynical statement by a conquering power. In fact, the commission found that only 10 percent of the population was literate. Both the commission's report and the later actions by the commissioners of education were undertaken in the spirit of trying to help the Puerto Rican people. The problem was the assumption that U.S. institutions, customs, and beliefs were the best in the world and that they should be imposed. The attempt to help was accompanied by an attitude of moral and cultural superiority.

During his short tenure (1900–1901), Brumbaugh began the process of Americanization. In a letter to school supervisors, he stated, "No school has done its duty unless it has impressed devout patriotism upon the hearts and minds of all the children."[8] He recruited teachers from the United States. Most of these teachers spoke only English, which meant that by default their instruction was not bilingual. Every school on the island was given an American flag, with most of them being donated by the Lafayette Post, Army of the Republic, New York City. The raising of the U.S. flag was used to signal the commencement of classes. Patriotic exercises were organized in the school with children being taught U.S. national songs such as "America," "Hail, Columbia," and "The Star-Spangled Banner."[9]

Therefore, within only four years of being an autonomous nation, Puerto Rican children were being educated to shift their allegiance from Puerto Rico to another country. The introduction of George Washington's birthday as a school holiday was part of this process. Schools were told to impress on students Washington's "noble traits and broad statesmanship." Exercises were organized which consisted of singing U.S. patriotic songs and reading Washington's speeches. In San Juan, 25,000 students were involved in the celebration. In Brumbaugh's words, "These exercises have done much to Americanize the island, much more than any other single agency."[10]

Letters were sent to teachers instructing them to celebrate, on June 14, 1901, the creation of the U.S. flag. Teachers were instructed to engage students in a celebration of the flag beginning with a flag salute followed by the singing of the U.S. national anthem. After this opening exercise, teachers were instructed to have students give speeches, recitations, and patriotic readings and to sing patriotic songs and march to band music.

Learning English was considered an important part of the Americanization process. In any language are embedded the customs and values of a particular culture. Similar to American Indians, Puerto Ricans were taught English to build patriotism. In his annual report, Brumbaugh states, "The first English many of them knew was that of our national songs."[11] While many teachers from the United States were not capable of conducting bilingual instruction, Brumbaugh believed that Spanish should be taught along with English. But, Brumbaugh believed, teachers from the United States should be placed in kindergarten and elementary schools to begin English instruction as early as possible.

During Brumbaugh's tenure Puerto Rican resistance to U.S. educational policies began to appear in the magazine *La Educación*

Moderna in a 1900 article, "English in the Schools." The article attacked "the spirit of . . . supremacy with which the English language is being imposed."[12]

The second commissioner of education, Samuel Lindsay (1902–1904), introduced more policies designed to educate Puerto Rican children into the U.S. way of life. An important part of his program was sending Puerto Rican teachers and students to the United States to learn the English language and U.S. culture. These trips were designed to prepare Puerto Rican teachers to teach about the United States when they returned to the classroom.[13] Combined with the patriotic celebrations initiated during Brumbaugh's tenure, the program of study abroad was intended to inculcate the values of the dominant society in the United States.

Lindsay also began to tighten policies regarding the teaching of English. First, he included an examination in English as part of the general examination for gaining a teacher's certificate.[14] Consider the impact of this requirement in the context of your own country. Imagine you were a teacher and suddenly, within four years of conquest, you were being examined on your knowledge of the language of the conquering country!

The language issue was taken one step further by Lindsay's successor, Roland Falkner. Falkner's impact on language policies extended far beyond his term, from 1904 to 1907. Falkner ordered that all instruction past the first grade be conducted in English. Of course, the major problem he encountered was that most Puerto Rican teachers did not know enough English to conduct instruction in that language. Consequently, as an incentive to improve their English skills, Falkner ordered that teachers be classified according to their scores on the English examination. In addition, the government provided English instruction for Puerto Rican teachers. Of course, it was impossible to convert an entire school system from one language to another in a short time, and therefore the results of the language policy were very spotty.

In addition, the journal *La Educación Moderna* launched an attack on the language policies. One Puerto Rican teacher complained in the journal that the instruction given by American teachers and that given by Puerto Rican teachers in English was having a disastrous effect on the students. The newspaper *La Democracia* editorialized that nothing could be done about the situation until the Department of Education was controlled by Puerto Ricans.[15]

While the language issue continued as a source of friction between Puerto Rican teachers and U.S. authorities, the next commissioner of education, Edwin Dexter (1907–1912), tried to increase the significance of patriotic celebrations in the schools. Although the Fourth of July was not a date in the school calendar, Dexter dressed a group of schoolchildren in red, white, and blue and marched them through the streets of San Juan under a large patriotic banner. Also, Dexter considered the celebration of Washington's and Lincoln's birthdays and Memorial Day to be an important means of teaching English because all events were conducted in that language. Adding to these activities, Dexter introduced military drill into the schools.[16]

In 1912, Puerto Rican teachers organized the Teachers Association to resist the policies of the commissioner of education. A teacher's magazine, *La Educación Moderna*, heralded the event: "Day after day we have worked for the defense of our mother tongue and at last today we see our efforts and publicity crowned with success by the meeting of the Teachers Association."[17]

During the term of Commissioner of Education Edward Bainter (1912–1915), the Teachers Association started to campaign to resume teaching in Spanish. The organization passed a resolution calling for the teaching of arithmetic in Spanish. In 1914, the organization requested that Spanish be used as the language of instruction in the first four years of grammar school with English being taught as a subject.

In 1915, resistance to the imposition of English sparked a student strike at Central High School in San Juan. The strike occurred when a student, Francisco Grovas, was expelled for collecting signatures to support legislation that would require Spanish to be the language of instruction in the Puerto Rican schools. This caused Commissioner of Education Paul Miller (1915–1921) to proclaim that any student participating in a strike would be suspended from school indefinitely.[18]

The strike at Central High School reflected a rising wave of nationalism and calls for independence. By 1915, Puerto Ricans were divided over the issues of independence and U.S. citizenship. The debate over citizenship was sparked by the introduction of legislation into the U.S. Congress to grant citizenship to Puerto Ricans. Speaking before the House of Representatives in 1916, Puerto Rican leader Muñoz Rivera requested that Congress let the Puerto Rican people vote as to whether or not they wanted U.S. citizenship. Ignoring this plea, Congress passed the Jones Act, which was signed into law by President Woodrow Wilson in 1917.[19]

The Jones Act obligated Puerto Ricans to serve in the U.S. military while denying them the right to vote in national elections. Similar to the Native Americans in Indian Territory, who were granted citizenship in 1901 as part of the process of abolishing tribal governments, many Puerto Ricans did not welcome this grant of citizenship.

Despite the imposition of citizenship, students and other groups continued to campaign for independence. One dramatic outbreak of nationalism occurred in 1921 during graduation exercises at Central High School when a student orator waved a Puerto Rican flag and cheered for independence. Commissioner Miller responded by ordering the removal of "the enemy flag" from the auditorium. Students responded that if the flag were removed, they would leave the ceremonies.[20]

Tensions increased in the 1920s with the appointment of the first Puerto Rican to the post of commissioner of education. As commissioner from 1921 to 1930, Juan B. Huyke imposed Americanization programs with a vengeance. Appointed because he favored assimilation to the United States in contrast to independence, Huyke called the independence movement unfortunate and stated his belief that it would shortly disappear from the minds of Puerto Ricans. He considered Puerto Rico to be "as much a part of the United States as is Ohio or Kentucky."[21] Defining Americanism as patriotism, "He that does not want to be a teacher of Americanism would do well not to follow me in my work."[22]

Committed to Americanization, Huyke resisted attempts to return to Spanish as the language of instruction. Huyke required that all high school seniors pass an oral English examination before they could graduate. School newspapers written in Spanish were banned. English became the required language at teachers' meetings, and teachers were asked to use English in informal discussions with students. School rankings were based on students' performance on English examinations. Student clubs were established to promote the speaking of English. Teachers who were unable or unwilling to use English in instruction were asked to resign.[23]

Similar to his predecessors, Huyke linked the ability to speak English to the learning of patriotism. This was exemplified by the creation of a School Society for the Promotion and Study of English

Language for all eighth-, ninth-, and tenth-graders in Puerto Rico. Supporting patriotism and English, society members were required to wear small American flags in their buttonholes and speak only English. For the celebration of American Education Week in 1921, Huyke recommended as a topic for a speech "American Patriotism—wear the flag in your heart as well as in your buttonhole."[24] In the monthly publication of the Department of Education of Puerto Rico, *Puerto Rico School Review*, Huyke summarized the attitudes about the role of the school in the colonialization of Puerto Rico: "Our schools are agencies of Americanism. They must implant the spirit of America within the hearts of our children."[25]

Resistance to Huyke's policies came from the Puerto Rican Teachers Association and students. The Teachers Association protested the lack of material on Puerto Rico in the curriculum and the failure to recognize Puerto Rican holidays and celebrations in the school calendar. They complained about the fact that out of the seventeen high school principals in Puerto Rico, only five were Puerto Rican. And, of course, they protested the English-language policies. Protest marches by university students were branded by Huyke as "aggressively anti-American" and students were expelled. Professors were warned to stop their support of the protests or resign their positions.[26]

Increasing protests over school policies eventually resulted in the Padin Reform of 1934, which restricted English-language instruction to high school and made content instruction in the upper elementary grades in Spanish. But textbooks remained in English. During the 1930s, President Franklin D. Roosevelt urged a bilingual policy with a stress on the importance of learning English. In Roosevelt's words, "But bilingualism will be achieved . . . only if the teaching of English . . . is entered into at once with vigor, purposefulness, and devotion, and with the understanding that English is the official language of our country."[27]

In 1946, the Teachers Association was able to pressure the Puerto Rican legislature into passing a bill requiring that instruction in public schools be given in Spanish. President Harry Truman vetoed the bill. From the perspective of many Puerto Ricans, the language issue could be resolved only by giving the island more political autonomy. On October 30, 1950, President Truman signed the Puerto Rican Commonwealth Bill, which provided for a plebiscite to determine whether Puerto Rico should remain a colony or become a commonwealth. In 1951, Puerto Ricans voted for commonwealth status despite protests by those urging Puerto Rican independence. Commonwealth status gave Puerto Ricans greater control of their school systems, and consequently Spanish was restored in the schools.[28]

CONCLUSION: METHODS OF DECULTURALIZATION AND AMERICANIZATION

The educational policies following the conquest of Native American tribes, Mexico, and Puerto Rico provide a guide to methods of deculturalization and Americanization. In many instances, these methods were not very effective. Despite the educational programs of the schools, all three groups maintained their cultural traditions. In part, the limited success of deculturalization might have been a result of resistance to these programs. Native Americans and Puerto Ricans struggled to pass on their traditions and languages to their children and resisted attempts at deculturalization.

It could be that deculturalization programs are self-defeating. When parents and children resist attempts to strip them of their cultural heritage, they might also resist other educational programs. In other words, deculturalization programs might turn both parents and children against all educational programs offered by schools. For instance, consider the dramatic decline in literacy among the Five Civilized Tribes after their schools were taken over by the state of Oklahoma. Under tribal leadership, the schools reflected native culture. Under the control of the state of Oklahoma, deculturalization programs resulted in a dramatic decline in literacy among the next generation of Indians.

On the other hand, Americanization programs might have been more effective. Native Americans and Puerto Ricans served in the military and fought in World War II and later wars. On the other hand, many Native Americans and Puerto Ricans still cling to nationalist sentiments. At the time of my father's death, the Great Seal of the Choctaw Nation—which is now on the Oklahoma state flag—hung prominently on his living room wall. Born in 1903 in Indian Territory, my father at birth had citizenship in both the Choctaw Nation and the United States. Symbolically, this dual citizenship represents the divided loyalty still felt by many Native Americans and Puerto Ricans.

Therefore, the educational programs for deculturalization and Americanization had mixed results. In general, deculturalization programs have used the following educational methods.

Methods of Deculturalization

1. Segregation and isolation
2. Forced change of language
3. Content of curriculum reflects culture of dominant group
4. Content of textbooks reflects culture of dominant group
5. Dominated groups are not allowed to express their culture and religion
6. Use of teachers from dominant group

The first method of deculturalization—segregation and isolation—was used with Native Americans. Indians sent to Indian Territory were isolated in the hope that missionary-educators would "civilize" them in one generation. Indian children sent to boarding schools were isolated from the cultural traditions of their tribe as they were "civilized."

Forcing a dominated group to abandon its own language is an important part of deculturalization. Culture and values are embedded in language. Educational policymakers in the nineteenth and early twentieth centuries believed that substituting English for Native American languages and for Spanish was the key to deculturalization. But the language issue created the greatest resistance by dominated groups. In fact, the attempt to change the languages of the groups under consideration may have been the major cause of the limited effectiveness of deculturalization programs.

Using a curriculum and textbooks that reflect the culture of the dominating group was a typical practice of state school systems and federal educational programs. Native Americans and Puerto Ricans attended schools where the curriculum and textbooks reflected the culture of the dominant white culture of the United States. The hope was that these groups would emulate the culture reflected in the curriculum and textbooks.

In boarding schools, Native American children were not allowed to practice their cultural traditions or their native religions. In Puerto Rican schools, the cultural bias of the curriculum and textbooks left little room for Puerto Rican culture. In both cases, the result might have been to alienate the children from the school.

And last, the use of teachers who represented the dominant culture was considered an important means of deculturalization. Missionary-educators and teachers from the Bureau of Indian Affairs were supposed to represent "civilization" to Native American children. Teachers brought from the United States to Puerto Rico were supposed to be cultural role models.

All of these methods of deculturalization were accompanied by programs of Americanization. Basically, these programs were designed to create emotional attachments to symbols of the U.S. government. In the case of Native Americans and Puerto Ricans, Americanization programs were supposed to change the loyalty of these people from their tribal governments or, in the case of Puerto Rico, from their nationalistic traditions to the U.S. government. The basic program for creating these emotional attachments included:

1. Flag ceremonies (one of the first methods used with Indian tribes and Puerto Ricans)
2. Replacement of local heroes with U.S. national heroes in school celebrations
3. Patriotic celebrations
4. Focusing the study of history on the traditions of the dominant white culture of the United States

The attempts at deculturalization were eventually countered in the 1950s and 1960s by the great civil rights movement. The strong resistance to deculturalization during the great civil rights movement highlights the difficulty, if not impossibility, of deculturalization through educational institutions.

NOTES

1. Ivan Musicant, *The Banana Wars: A History of the United States Military Intervention in Latin America from the Spanish-American War to the Invasion of Panama* (New York: Macmillan, 1990), p. 2.
2. As quoted in Aida Negron De Montilla, *Americanization in Puerto Rico and the Public-School System 1900–1930* (Rio Piedras: Editorial Edil, 1971), p. 62.
3. Ibid., pp. 6–79.

4. Negron De Montilla, pp. xi–xii.
5. Ibid., p. 37.
6. Ibid., pp. 35–36.
7. Ibid., p. 36.
8. Ibid., p. 51.
9. Ibid., pp. 47–48.
10. Ibid., p. 49.
11. Ibid., p. 48.
12. Ibid., p. 58.
13. Ibid., pp. 63–64.
14. Ibid., p. 71.
15. Ibid., pp. 105–106.
16. Ibid., pp. 121–123.
17. Ibid., p. 135.
18. Ibid., pp. 140, 170.
19. Ibid., p. 163.
20. Ibid., pp. 172–173.
21. Ibid., p. 178.
22. Ibid., p. 180.
23. Ibid., pp. 260–261.
24. Ibid., p. 183.
25. Ibid., p. 181.
26. Ibid., p. 187.
27. Catherine Walsh, *Pedagogy and the Struggle for Voice: Issues of Language, Power, and Schooling for Puerto Ricans* (New York: Bergin & Garvey, 1991), p. 20.
28. Ibid., pp. 20–21.

CHAPTER 4

Education and Segregation: African Americans

Segregation in public schools in the United States is directly related to maintaining an inexpensive source of labor. For instance, in the late nineteenth and early twentieth centuries, Japanese, Chinese, and Korean immigrants worked at low wages on railroads, in factories, and on farms, while, at the same time, their children were being segregated from European American children in California schools. In the South, segregated education was justified as providing an inexpensive source of workers for industrialization and the maintenance of agriculture. With the great migration of Mexicans as farm workers in the early twentieth century, segregated schools were created to assure that their children would also become migrant farm workers.

This relationship between segregated schools and economic exploitation was based on several factors. One factor was that segregated schools provided an inferior (as compared to schools serving European Americans) education. This made it difficult for economically exploited groups to use education as a means of economic advancement. The second factor was that many segregated students were taught to believe they were inferior, and, therefore, many accepted an inferior economic status. Of course, there were many segregated students who resisted that brand of inferiority and, later in life, fought schools' segregation. The third factor was that segregated education tended to emphasize the inculcation of habits and values required for menial employment. And last, segregated education tended to reinforce among many European Americans a belief in their own superiority. This feeling of superiority helped to rationalize economic exploitation. Believing in their own racial superiority, many European Americans could continue to pay low wages and to accept the squalid living conditions of these groups without feeling a sense of guilt. European Americans could say to themselves, "This is the only way these people know how to live. They should be grateful for what I give them."

BEFORE THE CIVIL WAR

The history of African-American education is highlighted by both the denial of education in order to continue economic exploitation and the use of segregated education to assure an inexpensive source of labor. Before the Civil War, the ability to attend school created important differences between enslaved Africans in southern states and freed Africans living in northern states. Enslaved Africans in the South were denied an education by law. It was feared that education would create the potential for rebellion among enslaved Africans. Between 1800 and 1835, southern states passed laws making it a crime to educate slaves. According to historian Henry Bullock, among white southerners there was a "general fear that literacy would expose the slaves to abolition literature."[1]

Some enslaved Africans were given a limited education in skilled occupations, such as carpentry and mechanics. However, this education was narrowly limited to training for particular occupations and did not offer any instruction that might threaten white control. Of course, any education nonetheless has the potential to provide tools that lead to demands for freedom.

Despite laws forbidding educating slaves, by the outbreak of the Civil War in 1860, 5 percent of slaves had learned how to read, sometimes literally at the risk of life or limb. Individual slaves would sneak books and teach themselves while hiding from their masters. Sometimes self-taught slaves would pass on their skills and knowledge to other slaves. James Anderson quotes a former slave, Ferebe Rogers, about her husband's educational work prior to the Civil War: "On his dyin' bed he said he been de death o' many a nigger 'cause he taught so many to read and write."[2]

Therefore, because of laws prohibiting education, the African-American culture that emerged from slavery was primarily based on an oral tradition and was centered around coping with the brutal institution of slavery. While coming from a variety of African cultures, enslaved Africans did share an African heritage and the culture they created in the context of slavery. To fully appreciate the culture created in slavery, one must consider the initial conditions faced by slaves. Transported to the Americas, slaves were put into conditions in which all of their accustomed modes of social interaction no longer existed. For instance, accustomed modes of marriage, family relations, property, child rearing, friendships, and social status were destroyed in the process of enslavement. Literally, enslaved Africans created their own modes of social interaction within the context of domination and enslavement.

In the words of anthropologists Sidney Mintz and Richard Price, "The Africans in any New World colony in fact became a community and began to share a culture insofar as, and as fast as, they themselves created them."[3] This culture had two important aspects. One aspect was the relationship among slaves. Another aspect was the relationship to the owner or master.

The intersection of slave culture and European-American culture was in the context of a master-slave relationship. Slaves had to learn and develop modes of interaction with a master who literally had the power of life and death; a master who could at anytime inflict severe punishment. It was a relationship in which the slave was not protected by any legal institution from the arbitrary brutality of the master and the owner could demand sexual relations with any slave. The owner had the power to break up families and wrench children from their parents by selling them.[4]

The oral tradition that developed among enslaved Africans provided a psychological refuge against the degradation of slavery. Slave songs were created while working, during whatever leisure time was available, and during religious services. The lyrics reflect the effort by slaves to create a culture that could cope with inhuman conditions. In fact, as I stated before, they had no other alternative than to create their own culture since they were denied acculturation to the surrounding European-American culture. In *Black Culture and Black Consciousness: Afro-American Folk Thought from Slavery to Freedom*, Lawrence Levine concludes, "The slaves' oral traditions, their music, and their religious outlook . . . constituted a cultural refuge at least potentially capable of protecting their personalities from some of the worst ravages of the slave system."[5]

Created in context of domination, this oral tradition reflected an obvious distrust and dislike of whites. It also contained a hope that in the end the slave would triumph over the master. Also, this oral tradition reflects the methods by which slaves tried to cope with their state of powerlessness. The religious songs of slaves often portrayed whites as the devil and slaves as the chosen people. As the chosen people, slaves would eventually triumph over the cruelties of white people. "We are the people of God," "we are de people of the Lord," "I really do believe I'm a child of God," "To the promised land I'm bound to go," and "Heaven shall-a be my home" are examples of refrains that ran through slave spirituals. On the other side of the coin, slave attitudes toward whites ranged from "You no holy. We be holy" to "No white people went to heaven."[6]

In relations with masters and other whites, slave tales outline a social system based on trickery. The only method the slave had for self protection was to try and trick the master. Within the ethical system of slavery, a slave did not consider taking something that was forbidden from the master as stealing. For instance, inadequate food was a constant problem for slaves. The reasoning of the slave was that taking food from the master was not stealing since the master owned the slave and the food consumed by the slave remained in the ownership of the master. On the other hand, taking something from a fellow slave was considered theft and the act was considered to be "just as mean as white folks."[7]

Typical of the slave as trickster was the story of Henry Johnson who lured a turkey into his cabin and killed it. He immediately ran crying to his mistress that one of her turkeys unexpectedly died. She told him to stop crying and get rid of the possibly diseased bird. That night Henry ate the turkey. In another story, a slave ran to his master to tell him that all seven of his hogs died. When the master appeared at the scene, a group of slaves informed him with sorrow that the hogs had died of "malitis" and that they were afraid to touch the meat. Reacting with fear for his own health at the word "malitis," the master ordered the slaves to eat the dead hogs. "Malitis," a word the slaves created, resulted from a slave hitting each hog in the head with a heavy mallet. In another story, a slave takes some chickens and begins cooking them in his cabin. The master enters the cabin and the slave informs him that he is cooking a possum. The master decides to wait and share the possum. Fearing that the master will discover the chickens, the slave tells him that it will take a long time to cook because slaves make their possum gravy by having the family spit in it. In disgust, the master leaves and the slaves eat the chickens. The animal tales provide a similar picture of the weak outsmarting the more powerful.[8]

The African-American culture that emerged from slavery was an oral culture of songs and stories that often depicted the culture of European Americans as inhuman, cold, and untrustworthy. A similar cultural attitude emerged among freed Africans in northern states who, while not enslaved, still faced discrimination, segregation, and white violence.

While the African-American population in northern states was only 225,000 by 1860, which represented 1 percent of the total population, white northerners saw them as a threat to their racial purity. Attempts to prohibit interracial marriages occurred in New York, Pennsylvania, Indiana, Wisconsin, and Illinois. Discrimination and segregation occurred throughout the north. In Philadelphia, African Americans were only allowed to ride on the front platforms of horse-drawn streetcars and in New York City blacks could only ride on "colored-only" vehicles. Race riots broke out in Philadelphia and Cincinnati. In 1834, rioting whites in Philadelphia forced blacks to flee and in 1841 whites in Cincinnati used a cannon against blacks defending their homes.[9]

In resisting efforts at discrimination and segregation, African Americans in northern states, unlike their enslaved brethren in the South, were able to militantly struggle for educational opportunities. While the culture of enslaved Africans contributed music and stories of resistance to oppression, freed African Americans created a culture of resistance focused on literacy, political action, and judicial solutions. After the Civil War these two cultural traditions blended into a steady struggle for civil rights that reached a high point in the great civil rights movement of the 1950s and 1960s. Therefore, the roots of African-American struggles for equal educational opportunity can be found in the early nineteenth century.

An important example of the early struggle for equality of educational opportunity occurred in Boston. Boston organized the first comprehensive system of urban schools after the passage of the Massachusetts Education Act of 1789. This legislation required towns to provide elementary schools for six months of the year and grammar schools in communities with more than 200 families. In 1790, the black population in Boston was 766 out of a total population of 18,038. At the beginning of the nineteenth century, no law or tradition excluded black children from the public schools. Some were enrolled in public schools, while others attended private ones.[10]

However, very few black children actually attended school. The low attendance rate was a result of the poor economic conditions of the black population and the hostile reception given black children in the public schools. To protect their children from the prejudice of white children, a committee of African Americans in 1798 asked for a separate system of schools for their children. The Boston School Committee rejected this request with the reasoning that if it provided separate schools for blacks, it would also need to provide separate schools for other groups. Receiving aid from white philanthropists, the parents opened a school that survived for only a few months. In 1800, a group of thirty-six African Americans again asked the Boston School Committee to establish a separate school for their children. Again the answer was no. Two years later the black community opened another separate private school.[11]

In 1806, the school committee reversed its position and opened a segregated school with a combination of public funds and contributions from white philanthropists. In 1812, the school committee voted permanent funds for the school and established direct control over it.[12]

The Boston School Committee's decision created a complex situation. First, the committee supported and controlled a segregated school, although no law existed requiring segregation. In theory at least, black children were free to attend public schools other than the one established for them. Second, the African-American community supported the segregated school as an alternative to the prejudice existing in the other white-dominated schools. And last, the school was supported by a combination of private and public monies. Private contributions to the school became a major factor when Abiel Smith died in 1815 and left the entire income for his shares in New England turnpikes and bridges and from the U.S. bonds he had owned to the support of black schools. The school committee assumed trusteeship of the estate, which meant that it controlled both the school and the majority of private funds supporting the school.[13]

By the 1820s, the African-American community realized that a segregated education was resulting in an inferior education for their children. The school committee was appointing inferior teachers to the all-black school and was not maintaining the school building. In 1833, a subcommittee issued a report on the conditions of the schools. The major conclusion of this report was that black schools were inferior to other schools in both the quality of education and the physical conditions. The report argued that "a classroom better than a basement room in the African Church could be found. After all, Black parents paid taxes which helped to support white schools. They deserved a more equal return on their share of the city's income."[14]

The most important conclusion of the report was that segregated education was not benefiting either race. The Boston School Committee responded to the report by focusing efforts on building a new segregated school. The school committee accepted the idea of segregated education and argued that the real problem was assuring that separate schools for black children were equal to those of whites.

In contrast, the African-American community responded to the report by questioning the whole idea of segregation and asking the important question: Could segregated schools ever be equal?

Local black abolitionist, David Walker, answered this question with a resounding "No!" Walker was representative of an increasingly militant and literate African-American community in the northern states. Walker was born in North Carolina in 1779 of a free mother and a slave. According to North Carolina law, Walker was thus born free. He moved to Boston in the early 1820s and became a contributor to and local agent for the nation's first black newspaper, *Freedom's Journal*, published in New York.

In the newspaper and in his other writings, Walker argued that there were four principal factors responsible for the poor situation of blacks in the nation: slavery; the use of religion to justify slavery and prejudice; the African colonization movement designed to send free blacks back to Africa; and the lack of educational opportunity. White Americans, he argued, were keeping black Americans from receiving any significant amount of education. As proof, he cited the laws in the South that made it illegal to educate slaves. In the North, according to Walker, the inferior education blacks received in schools was designed to keep them at a low level of education.[15]

After studying the conditions in Boston schools, Walker reached the conclusion that segregated education in the city was a conspiracy by whites to keep blacks in a state of ignorance. Walker's arguments added fuel to the fire. Demands by the black community for integrated education intensified, and for almost two decades the black community struggled with the school committee to end segregated education. Part of the issue was the loss of control of black schools by the black community. Originally, the black community exercised control over its early private educational endeavors. Over the years, however, the school committee had gained complete control, so that any complaints the black community had about its schools had to be resolved by the committee.

In 1849, the protests over segregated schools finally reached the Massachusetts Supreme Judicial Court when Benjamin Roberts sued the city for excluding his five-year-old daughter from the schools. In this particular case, his daughter passed five white primary schools before reaching the black school. Consequently, Roberts decided to enroll her in one of the closer white schools. He lost the case on a decision by the court that the school system had provided equal schools for black children. This was one of the first separate-but-equal rulings in American judicial history.

The issue of segregation in Massachusetts schools was finally resolved in 1855, when the governor signed into law a requirement that no child be denied admission to a public school on the basis of race or religious opinions. In September of that year the Boston public schools were integrated without any violent hostilities.

This early history of segregated education illustrates the growing willingness of the African-American community to use political action and the courts to gain equal educational opportunity. It also illustrates that African-American culture was forming around reaction to the racism and prejudice of whites.

The Boston situation also illustrates the ambivalent attitudes of whites about the education of African Americans. On the one hand, whites might feel that containing the threat of African culture to the dominant Protestant culture of the United States required "civilizing" African Americans in the same manner as Native Americans. This meant providing schools. On the other hand, whites who considered Africans a threat to their racial purity and culture, and who believed Africans were "inferior," wanted the "civilizing" or education of African Americans to occur in segregated schools. As a result of the latter beliefs, public education for African Americans in the United States remained primarily segregated in the nineteenth and twentieth centuries.

THE GREAT CRUSADE FOR LITERACY

Despite school segregation and harassment from the white population, the African-American population of the United States made one of the greatest educational advancements in the history of education. Denied an education by law in slave states and facing inequality of educational opportunities in free states, only 7 percent, as indicated by Table 1, of the African-American population was literate in 1863. This 7 percent was composed mainly of free African Americans in Northern states. A small part of this 7 percent was composed of enslaved Africans who broke laws to become literate. As indicated in Table 1, within a 90-year period, the literacy rate jumped to 90 percent.

After the Civil War, former slaves struggled to establish schools, and in many cases they were assisted by teachers from the North. In Reconstruction conventions following the Civil War, blacks fought for the establishment of state school systems. In the words of W. E. B. Du Bois, "Public education for all at public expense was, in the South, a Negro idea."[16] In the early 1870s, black children were enrolled in school systems at percentages higher than those for whites, but by the 1800s this situation began to change as whites exerted greater control over the state political systems and passed dis-

TABLE 1. Decline in Illiteracy in the Adult African-American Population of the United States

Date	% Illiterate
1863	93
1870	80
1890	56
1900	44
1910	30
1920	23
1930	16
1940	11
1950	10

[1] This table was adapted from Lawrence W. Levine, *Black Culture and Black Consciousness: Afro-American Folk Thought from Slavery to Freedom* (New York: Oxford University Press, 1977), p. 156.

criminatory laws. By the 1890s, as a consequence of sharecropping and other forms of economic exploitation and discriminatory laws, many blacks found themselves living in conditions that were close to slavery.

During and immediately after the Civil War, former slaves took the initiative in establishing schools. The first of these efforts was made by a black teacher, Mary Peake, who organized a school in 1861 at Fortress Monroe, Virginia.[17] The role of freed slaves in establishing schools was recorded by the first national superintendent of schools for the Freedman's Bureau, John W. Alvord. Based on his travels through the South in 1865, Alvord's first general report for the Freedman's Bureau in 1866 described former slaves' efforts at self-education. Everywhere in the South, he found ex-slaves studying elementary textbooks. He described a school in North Carolina organized by two freed slaves with 150 students in attendance. An illustration in *Harper's Weekly* in 1866 showed a large classroom full of freed slaves and a black teacher in the Zion School in Charleston, South Carolina. The administrators and teachers of the school were all African Americans, and the average daily attendance was 720 students.[18]

By the middle of the 1870s, differing ideas on education were struggling for dominance in the South. Because of their need for children as farm laborers, planters resisted most attempts to expand educational opportunities for black children. On the other hand, former slaves were struggling for an education that would improve their economic and political positions in southern society. In contrast to these two positions, there were groups of white southerners who believed that the expansion of education was necessary for the industrialization of the South. These white southerners supported schooling for African Americans as a means of teaching them industrial habits and keeping them on the lowest rungs of southern society. For those southerners who supported industrialization, blacks represented a potential source of cheap labor who, unlike northern workers, would not form unions.

Within the black community in the 1890s, divisions developed over how to pursue the struggle for education. This division is most often associated with two major black leaders—Booker T. Washington and W. E. B. Du Bois. Washington accepted compromise with white demands and the establishment of segregated industrial education; Du Bois maintained that no compromise with white demands should be made and that black education should be concerned with educating the future leaders of the black community. To a certain extent, however, the preceding statements oversimplify both their positions. Their hopes for schooling were interwoven with their hopes for their race, the realities of southern society, and their political strategies. In the history of schooling, Washington is most often associated with the establishment of segregated schools, whereas Du Bois was instrumental in the founding in 1909 of the National Association for the Advancement of Colored People (NAACP), which has led the successful struggle against school segregation in the United States.

The speech that most clearly outlined the southern compromise and the role of blacks in the developing industrial order was given by Washington at the International Exposition in Atlanta in 1895. Washington tried to convince his all-white audience of the economic value of African Americans to the new industrial South by beginning his speech with a story about a ship lost at sea whose crew was dying of thirst. The ship encountered a friendly vessel, which signaled for the crew to cast down their buckets in the surrounding water. After receiving the signal four times, the captain finally cast down his bucket to find fresh water from the mouth of the Amazon River. This, Washington told his audience, was what the South needed to do to build its industrial might: cast down its buckets and use black workers. Washington continued his speech by outlining the advantages of black workers for the South. Of primary importance was that the South would not need to rely on foreign workers. "To those of the white race," Washington exclaimed, "who look to the incoming of those of foreign birth and strange tongue and habits for the prosperity of the South, were I permitted I would repeat what I say to my own race, 'Cast down your bucket where you are.'"[19] Washington continued by extolling the virtues of black workers and their faithfulness during the years of slavery. He claimed that blacks could show a devotion that no foreign workers would ever display and called for an interlacing of the interests of black and white southerners.

Then, in one sentence that would become famous in both the South and the North, Washington presented the compromise he saw as necessary for winning white southerners to his argument: "In all things that are purely social we can be as separate as the fingers, yet one as the hand in all things essential to mutual progress." Here was the great compromise—acceptance by blacks of social segregation for the opportunity to participate in the new industrial order of the South. As Washington explained in the conclusion of his speech, he believed that once the economic value of blacks had been established, social acceptance would follow. "No race," he argued, "that has anything to contribute to the markets of the world is long in any degree ostracized." In Washington's mind, "the opportunity to earn a dollar in a factory just now is worth infinitely more than the opportunity to spend a dollar in an opera-house."[20]

Washington believed that African Americans would be able to prove themselves economically by receiving the right form of education. Before that speech, Washington had received recognition throughout the South for his establishment of the Tuskegee Institute. The Tuskegee idea originated in Washington's educational experiences at the Hampton Institute. Washington had been born to slavery and after the Civil War attended Hampton, which had been established by General Samuel Armstrong, whose missionary parents had organized an industrial school for natives in Hawaii.

Washington was strongly influenced by General Armstrong's vision of the role of education in adjusting former slaves to their new place in the southern social order. Armstrong believed that the purpose of education was adjusting African Americans to a subordinate position in southern society. He also believed that blacks should be denied the right to vote and that they should be segregated; in short, that they should not be granted the same civil equality as whites.[21]

As part of the process of adjusting African Americans to permanent subordination in society, Armstrong argued that the primary purpose of educating African Americans was the development of "proper" work habits and moral behavior. This argument was based on a belief that "savages" were mentally capable but lacked a developed morality. Historian Anderson quotes Armstrong: "Most savage people are not like 'dumb driven cattle'; yet their life is little better than that of brutes because the moral nature is dormant."[22]

As Armstrong envisioned the process, Hampton graduates would become teachers who would educate the rest of the African-American population in the moral and work habits taught at Hampton. Taking its cue from attitudes regarding the education of Native Americans, Hampton was to be the agent for civilizing freed slaves. With Hampton teachers spread across the South, Armstrong believed, African Americans would be "civilized" and brought to accept their subordinate place in society.

The key to the civilizing process advocated by Armstrong and incorporated into Hampton's educational program was hard work. Armstrong believed that hard work was the first principle of civilized life. It was through hard work, according to Armstrong, that people learned the right moral habits. He believed that African Americans needed to be educated in the value of hard work if they were to assume their proper place in southern society.

Consequently, the curriculum at Hampton emphasized hard manual labor as part of teacher training. In addition, Armstrong believed that classical studies only developed vanity in black students and should not be part of the teacher-training curriculum for black students. Therefore, rather than studying the traditional liberal arts, Hampton male students worked in a sawmill, on the school farm, as dishwashers and busboys in the kitchen, as waiters in the dining room, and as houseboys in the living quarters. Hampton female students sewed, cooked, scrubbed, and plowed fields on the school's farm.[23]

Of course, according to many southern whites, the type of work performed by Hampton students was the type of work all African Americans should perform. In the context of Armstrong's larger philosophy, the occupational training at Hampton reflected the subordinated roles African Americans would play in the new economic order. By learning the habits and moral values associated with doing these tasks, Hampton graduates, Armstrong believed, would teach other African Americans the habits and values required to make these tasks lifelong occupations.

Therefore, when General Armstrong and Booker T. Washington used the term "industrial education," they primarily meant the development of good work and moral habits as opposed to learning a particular vocational skill. For instance, historian James Anderson in his history of black education reproduces photographs of prospective female teachers at Hampton plowing and tilling a farm field. Obviously, these future teachers were not being educated to be farmers. But they were learning the work habits that Armstrong wanted his graduates to pass on to their students.

It was Armstrong's philosophy of education that guided Washington in the establishment of Tuskegee. Washington scorned the traditional forms of education brought south by northern teachers.

He felt that traditional education was useless and left the student with false promises for a better life. In his autobiography, *Up from Slavery*, he tells the story of mothers who taught their daughters the skill of laundering. "Later," Washington says, "these girls entered the public schools and remained there perhaps six or eight years. When the public-school course was finally finished, they wanted more costly dresses, more costly hats and shoes." Washington summarizes the effects of a traditional public school education: "In a word, while their wants had been increased, their ability to supply their wants had not been increased in the same degree. On the other hand, their six or eight years of book education had weaned them away from the occupation of their mothers." In another situation, Washington criticizes a young man fresh out of high school who "sitting down in a one-room cabin, with grease on his clothing, filth all round him, and weeds in the yard and garden, engaged in studying French grammar."[24] Washington's message was heard throughout the North and South. It was particularly welcomed by those trying to organize the southern school system. The idea of segregated industrial education that stressed proper moral and work habits also received support from major educational conferences and private foundations. It was this support that made segregated education a permanent fixture in southern states until the 1950s and 1960s. In Henry Bullock's words:

> The industrial curriculum to which many Negro children were exposed, supposedly designed to meet their needs, reflected the life that accompanied their status at that time. They had always farmed. The curriculum aimed to make them better farmers. Negro women had a virtual monopoly on laundering, and Negro men had [worked] largely as mechanics. The industrial curriculum was designed to change this only in so far that Negroes were trained to perform these services better.[25]

As James Anderson tells the story, segregated industrial education as the model for black southern education received support from both southern industrialists and northern philanthropists. For instance, steel magnate and philanthropist Andrew Carnegie gave the first major endowment to Tuskegee because he believed that educating black workers was necessary to maintain the United States' position in the world economy. Carnegie stressed the importance of maintaining proper work habits among the black southern population. In comparing the black workforce in South Africa to that in the United States, Carnegie wrote, "We should be in the position in which South Africa is today but for the faithful, placable, peaceful, industrious, lovable colored man; for industriousness and peaceful he is compared with any other body of colored men on the earth."[26]

Indeed, southern industrialists welcomed the idea of segregated industrial education because it promised cheap labor and the avoidance of labor unions. One of the things Washington argued in his Atlanta speech was that the industrialists in the South had to choose between immigrant labor and black labor, and that the problem with immigrant laborers was that they formed labor unions. For instance, southern railroad magnate and Tuskegee supporter William H. Baldwin, Jr., argued that for the South to compete in international markets, it would have to reject the high wages demanded by white labor unions and rely upon the labor of African Americans.[27]

Despite the fact that some southern industrialists and educational leaders supported segregated industrial education for blacks, actual government financial support declined rapidly after the 1870s. In his classic study *The Education of the Negro in the American Social Order*, Horace Mann Bond collected information on school expenditures from a variety of southern states. For instance, a table illustrating spending in Alabama shows that in 1875–1876, expenditure per capita was actually higher for blacks than for whites. This relationship existed until the 1880s. By 1900 the situation had so far reversed that the per capita expenditure for whites was four to five times higher than that for blacks. Bond found similar statistics throughout the South.[28]

Therefore, by 1900, African Americans in the South faced a segregated public school system that made few expenditures for the education of their children. The major resistance to increased school expenditures for black students came from planters, who considered education a direct threat to their use of black children as agricultural laborers. As I will discuss in the next section of this chapter, the concerns of southern planters were similar to those expressed by farmers in Texas and California regarding the education of the children of Mexican-American farm workers. Southern planters foresaw the possibility that schooling would cause African Americans either to leave menial agricultural work or to demand higher wages. In addition, planters depended on the use of child labor and, consequently, opposed compulsory education laws. Some planters forced schools to begin their school year in December, after the harvest. In addition, they fought efforts to increase state financing of schools.[29]

By 1875, according to James Anderson, the planters' efforts resulted in halting the expansion of schools for African Americans in the South. Between 1880 and 1900, Anderson writes, "the number of black children of school age increased 25 percent, but the proportion attending public school fell."[30]

Consequently, by 1900 the dream of education for African Americans in the South was shattered as the majority of public expenditures went to support white segregated schools and large numbers of black children were kept working in the fields. In 1900, 49.3 percent of African-American boys between the ages of ten and fifteen were working, while 30.6 percent of the girls in the same age category were employed. The majority of these children, 404,225 out of 516,276, were employed as unskilled farm labor.[31] In the end, the segregation of public schools resulted in the denial of education to large numbers of black children.

RESISTING SEGREGATION

The major resistance to school segregation came from the NAACP, which has struggled for integrated education from its founding in 1909 to the present time. W. E. B. Du Bois, a founder of the NAACP and editor of the magazine *Crisis*, became the leading opponent of Booker T. Washington's southern compromise. Du Bois was born in Great Barrington, Massachusetts, earned a Ph.D. at Harvard, studied in Europe, and became one of America's leading sociologists. However, like most blacks in the late nineteenth and early twentieth centuries, he had difficulty finding a university teaching position. Some of his most famous studies were done while he taught at Atlanta University; *The Philadelphia Negro: A Social Study* was written with the support of the University of Pennsylvania but without an appointment to its faculty. One of his major public statements attacking the arguments of Booker T. Washington is *The Souls of Black Folk*, published in 1903.

In *The Souls of Black Folk*, Du Bois claims that Washington's compromise resulted in disaster for black people in the South: "Mr. Washington distinctly asks that black people give up, at least for the present, three things—First, political power, Second, insistence on civil rights, Third, higher education of Negro youth,—and concentrate all their energies on industrial education, the accumulation of wealth, and the conciliation of the South." The result, Du Bois argues, was the "disfranchisement of the Negro," the "legal creation of a distinct status of civil inferiority for the Negro," and the "steady withdrawal of aid from institutions for the higher education of the Negro."[32]

Du Bois envisioned a different type of education for blacks, one that would provide leaders to protect the social and political rights of the black community and make the black population aware of the necessity for constant struggle. He also wanted to develop an Afro-American culture that would blend the African background of former slaves with American culture. In part, this was to be accomplished by the education of black leaders.

What Du Bois hoped to accomplish through education is well described in his study of John. In the story, a southern black community raises money to send John to the North for an education. The community's hope is that he will return to teach in the local black school. After receiving his education in the North, John does return to teach. He goes to the house of the local white judge and, after making the mistake of knocking at the front door instead of the rear door, is ushered into the judge's dining room. The judge greets John with his philosophy of education: "In this country the Negro must remain subordinate, and can never expect to be [the] equal of white men." The judge describes two different ways in which blacks might be educated in the South. The first, which the judge favors, is to "teach the darkies to be faithful servants and laborers as your fathers were." The second way, the one supported by Du Bois and most feared by white Southerners, is described by the judge as putting "fool ideas of rising and equality into these folks' heads, and . . . [making] them discontent and unhappy."[33]

What was most important for Du Bois was to educate blacks to be discontented with their social position in the South. Unhappiness—not happiness—was his goal. Du Bois describes John, before his meeting with the judge, standing on a bluff with his younger sister and looking out over an expanse of water:

> Long they stood together, peering over the gray unsettled water.
> "John," she said, "does it make everyone unhappy when they study and learn lots of things?"

> He paused and smiled. "I am afraid it does," he said.
>
> "And, John, are you glad you studied?"
>
> "Yes," came the answer, slowly and positively.
>
> She watched the flickering lights upon the sea, and said thoughtfully, "I wish I was unhappy—and—and," putting both arms about his neck, "I think I am, a little, John."[34]

Du Bois's ideal of an educated black citizenry struggling against oppression became a reality even within a segregated society and educational system. Certainly, the combination of segregated education and the lack of funding of schools serving African Americans hindered the social and economic advancement of blacks. It took more than a half century for the NAACP to win its battle against segregated education in the South. During that period of legal struggle, segregated schooling was a major factor in condemning blacks to an inferior status in society.

THE SECOND CRUSADE

The first crusade for black education in the South took place during and after the Civil War, while the second crusade occurred from 1910 to the 1930s. The second crusade involved the expansion of segregated schools for African-American children paid for by a combination of personal donations of time and money by black citizens, donations by private foundations, and government money. It was through these efforts that by the 1930s common schools were finally established for black children. What is important to note about the second crusade is that black southern citizens had to pay directly from their own income to build schools for their children, while, at the same time, they paid local and state taxes, which went primarily to support white segregated schools.

One of the important private foundations supporting the second crusade was the Anna T. Jeanes Fund. The Jeanes Fund paid up to 84 percent of the salaries for teacher supervisors and elementary industrial education. The majority of the time of the Jeanes teachers, as they were popularly called, was spent in raising money for the construction of schoolhouses and the purchase of equipment. According the James Anderson, between 1913 and 1928, Jeanes teachers raised approximately $5 million. In this respect, Jeanes teachers played an important role in helping African Americans raise the money for black education that was being denied them by state and local governments dominated by white citizens.

The Julius Rosenwald Fund, named after its founder, Julius Rosenwald, the president of Sears, Roebuck and Company, led the campaign in building schools for black children. The first Rosenwald school was completed in 1914 in Lee County, Alabama. The construction of this one-teacher schoolhouse cost $942. Indicative of how the costs were being shared, impoverished local black residents donated $282 in cash and free labor. Local white citizens gave $360. The Rosenwald Fund gave $300.[35]

Between the building of the first Rosenwald school in 1914 and 1932, 4,977 rural black schools were constructed that could accommodate 663,615 students. The total expenditure for building these schools in 883 counties in fifteen southern states was $28,408,520. James Anderson provides the following breakdown for the financial sources of this massive building program: Rosenwald Fund—15.36 percent; rural black people—16.64 percent; white donations—4.27 percent; and public tax funds—63.73 percent.[36]

According to historian Anderson, the public tax funds used to build the Rosenwald schools came primarily from black citizens. In fact, he argues that the majority of school taxes collected from black citizens went to the support of schools for white children. Anderson writes, "During the period 1900 to 1920, every southern state sharply increased its tax appropriations for building schoolhouses, but virtually none of this money went for black schools."[37] Booker T. Washington complained, "The money [taxes] is actually being taken from the colored people and given to white schools."[38]

In reality, because of the source of funding, many of these public black schools were owned by local black citizens. One analysis of school expenditures in the South concluded that blacks owned 43.9 percent, or 1,816, of a total of 4,137 schools. Many of the schools identified as being in the public domain were paid for through the voluntary contributions of black citizens.[39]

Therefore, the second crusade for black education in the South involved a great deal of self-help from the black community. It was through the struggles and sacrifices of the black community that by the 1930s African-American children in the South had a viable system of education. Of course, the major drawback to this system was segregation and unequal financial support by state and local governments. Overcoming segregated education would require another period of activism by black citizens in the 1940s, 1950s, and 1960s.

NOTES

1. Henry Allen Bullock, *A History of Negro Education in the South: From 1619 to the Present* (New York: Praeger, 1970), p. 11.
2. James Anderson, *The Education of Blacks in the South 1860–1935* (Chapel Hill: University of North Carolina Press, 1988), p. 17.
3. Sidney Mintz and Richard Price, *The Birth of African American Culture* (Boston: Beacon Press, 1976), p. 14.
4. Toni Morrison captures the full psychological impact of this system in her Pulitzer Prize-winning novel *Beloved* (New York: Penguin Books, 1988).
5. Lawrence W. Levine, *Black Culture and Black Consciousness: Afro-American Folk Thought from Slavery to Freedom* (New York: Oxford University Press, 1977), p. 54.
6. Ibid., pp. 33–34.
7. Ibid., p. 125.
8. Ibid., pp. 81–135.
9. Ronald Takaki, *A Different Mirror: A History of Multicultural America* (Boston: Little, Brown and Company, 1933), pp. 106–138.
10. Stanley Schultz, *The Culture Factory: Boston Public Schools, 1789–1860* (New York: Oxford University Press, 1973).
11. Ibid.
12. Ibid.
13. Ibid.
14. Ibid., p. 169.
15. Quoted in ibid., p. 173.
16. Anderson, p. 6.
17. Ibid., p. 7.
18. Ibid., pp. 6–8.
19. Booker T. Washington, "Up from Slavery" in John Hope Franklin, ed., *Three Negro Classics* (New York: Avon Books, 1965), p. 147.
20. Ibid., p. 149.
21. Ibid., p. 36.
22. Anderson, p. 40.
23. Ibid., p. 55.
24. Washington, "Up from Slavery," pp. 77, 94.
25. Bullock, p. 88.
26. Quoted in Anderson, *Education of Blacks*, p. 91.

27. Ibid., pp. 90–91.
28. Horace Mann Bond, *The Education of the Negro in the American Social Order* (New York: Octagon Books, 1966), p. 153.
29. Ibid., pp. 22–23.
30. Ibid., p. 23.
31. Ibid., p. 149.
32. W. E. B. Du Bois, "The Souls of Black Folk" in Franklin, *Three Negro Classics*, pp. 246–247.
33. Ibid., p. 373.
34. Ibid., p. 372.
35. Ibid., p. 153.
36. Ibid.
37. Anderson, p. 156.
38. Quoted in ibid.
39. Ibid.

CHAPTER 5

Education as Segregation: Asian Americans and Mexican Americans

ASIAN AMERICANS

Asian Americans were the largest immigrant group affected by the Naturalization Act of 1790 which only allowed whites to become naturalized citizens. While Asian immigrants' children born in the United States were citizens, their parents could never achieve that status. According to the Naturalization Act of 1790, the "Founding Fathers" of the United States clearly stated their intentions that the country would be primarily composed of a white population.

During its more than 150 years of existence, the Naturalization Act of 1790 was used by members of federal and state governments to try and keep the population primarily white. The law denied U.S. citizenship to immigrants from Africa and Asia, and Native Americans. The law was used to deny Asian immigrants the right to own property. In the 1920s, laws were passed in California, Washington, Arizona, Oregon, Idaho, Nebraska, Texas, Kansas, Louisiana, Montana, New Mexico, Minnesota, and Missouri denying the right to own land to individuals who were ineligible for U.S. citizenship. The purpose of these laws was to deny land ownership to Asians, who, because of the Naturalization Act of 1790, were ineligible for citizenship.[1]

U.S. Supreme Court interpretations of the Naturalization Act of 1790 made it clear that race was primarily defined according to skin color. In denying citizenship to Chan Yong in 1855, a federal district court in California ruled that under the 1790 Naturalization Act citizenship was restricted to whites only.[2] In the early 1920s, a group of Asian Indians claimed they were eligible for citizenship because they were Caucasian. Previous rulings by the U.S. Supreme Court declared that the reference to "white person" in the Naturalization Act of 1790 was synonymous with Caucasian. This interpretation of the law was used to deny citizenship to Japanese immigrants. When Asian Indians argued in 1923 in *U.S.* v. *Bhagat Singh Thind* that they were Caucasian and therefore eligible for citizenship, the Supreme Court stated that while Asian Indians were Caucasians, they could not be considered a "white person." As the Supreme Court understood the term "white person," it meant an immigrant from Europe. The Supreme Court stated, "It may be true that the blond Scandinavian and the brown Hindu have a common ancestor in the dim reaches of antiquity, but the average man knows perfectly well that there are unmistakable and profound differences between them today."[3] The Court argued that "the intention of the Founding Fathers was to 'confer the privilege of citizenship upon the class of persons they knew as white.' "[4]

The hostility of whites was a rude surprise to Asian immigrants. Similar to other immigrants, they hoped to make their fortune in the United States and either return to their homelands or build a home in their new country. The first Chinese migrants arrived in California in the 1850s to join the rush for gold. In search of the Golden Mountain, these first arrivals were free laborers who paid their own transportation to the gold fields of California. By 1852, there were about 20,000 Chinese immigrants in California. By the 1860s, approximately 16,000 Chinese immigrants were working in the California gold fields. But as mining profits decreased, the Chinese immigrants found themselves without enough money to return to their homeland. Searching for work, these Chinese immigrants were hired to build the transcontinental railroad at wages that were about one-third less than would have been paid to a white worker. In addition, Chinese workers filled low wage jobs and built the agricultural industry in California.[5]

Feeling threatened by the rising Chinese-American population, whites sought to limit Chinese immigration through legislation. In 1878, John Miller expressed his fears at the California constitutional convention: "Were the Chinese to amalgamate at all with our people, it would be the lowest, most vile and degraded of our race, and the result of that amalgamation would be a hybrid of the most despicable, a mongrel of the most detestable that has ever afflicted the earth."[6] In response to these fears, Congress passed the Chinese Exclusion Act of 1882 which prohibited Chinese immigration.

Given these anti-Chinese and racist feelings among the dominant white population of California, it was not surprising that early school codes deliberately failed to mention Asian Americans, Native Americans, and African Americans. For instance, the California school code of 1872 states: "Every school, unless otherwise provided by special statute must be opened for the admission of *all white children* [the emphasis is mine] between five and twenty-one years residing in a district. . . ."[7]

The exclusion of Chinese from public education was challenged in 1884, when the Imperial Chinese Consulate complained to San Francisco school superintendent Andrew Moulder about the refusal of the school district to admit Mamie Tape. In this particular case, Mamie Tape was a Chinese American born in the United States and, therefore, had U.S. citizenship. The San Francisco School Board swiftly reacted to the complaint by adopting a resolution "That each and every principal of each and every public school . . . hereby absolutely prohibited from admitting any Mongolian child of schoolable age, or otherwise, either male or female, into such school or class."[8]

Reflecting the strong anti-Chinese feelings of white residents, the San Francisco Board of Supervisors responded to Mamie Tape's request to enter public schools: "Guard well the doors of our public schools that they [the Chinese] do not enter. For however stern it might sound, it is but the enforcement of the law of self-preservation, the inculcation of the doctrine of true humanity and an integral part of the iron rule of right by which we hope presently to prove that we can justly and practically defend ourselves from this invasion of Mongolian barbarism."[9]

On January 9, 1885, Superior Court Judge Maguire ruled in favor of Mamie Tape. Arguing that the Fourteenth Amendment to the Constitution guaranteed equal protection, including equal access to public schooling, Judge Maguire stated, "It would, moreover, be unjust to levy a forced tax upon Chinese residents to help maintain our schools, and yet prohibit their children born here from education in those schools."[10]

Obviously prepared for Maguire's decision, the California legislature on January 23, 1885, only two weeks after the decision, revised the California school code to provide education for Chinese children in "segregated" schools. The revised code gave local school boards the power "to establish separate schools for children of Mongolian or Chinese descent. When such separate schools are established Chinese or Mongolian children must not be admitted into any other school."[11]

On April 13, 1885, the segregated Chinese Primary School was opened at Jackson and Powell streets in San Francisco. Sacramento followed San Francisco's example and established a segregated school for Chinese in 1893. The rigid policy of segregation broke down by 1905, when the board of education had to let Chinese youths attend the regular city high school.

The establishment of segregated schools for Japanese children in California caused an international incident. Japanese immigrants did not enter California in large numbers until the early twentieth century. Although California employers saw Japan as a cheap source of Asian labor, anti-Asian hysteria greeted the Japanese, as it had the Chinese. While native whites worried about job competition and the resulting low wages, Japanese entered the country with expectations of becoming permanent citizens and with high educational standards. The Japanese, like the Chinese, were caught between American companies wanting to use cheap oriental labor and American workers who did not want the competition. In either case, arguments of racial inferiority and "yellow menace" were used to justify either exclusion from the United States or economic exploitation.

The resolution that segregated Japanese children in the San Francisco school district stated that segregation was "not only for the purpose of relieving the congestion at present prevailing in our schools, but also for the higher end that our children should not be placed in any position where their youthful impression may be affected by association with pupils of the 'Mongolian race.' " In 1906 the San Francisco Board of Education established a separate school for Chinese, Japanese, and Korean children. A majority of the Japanese parents boycotted the school, and the Japanese community then tried to win public opinion in Japan to its side as a means of forcing favorable action from the U.S. government. Editorials began to appear in Tokyo newspapers claiming that segregation was an insult to the nation, and in October 1906 the American ambassador to Japan warned the U.S. government of the developing international situation. The result was that President Theodore Roosevelt threatened the San Francisco school system with federal action if segregation did not end. However, the involvement of the federal government did not end segregation for the Japanese in other areas; they continued to face various exclusionary laws and legal actions through World War II.[12]

The segregation of Asian Americans illustrates the strong racist feelings existing among whites in the late nineteenth and early twentieth centuries. This racism, as reflected in the rhetoric of the time, was based on the same beliefs held by the "Founding Fathers" that the United States should be a primarily white nation. In addition, it was a continuation of the culture wars as Protestant Anglo-Americans tried to assure the continued domination of their culture.

MEXICAN AMERICANS

As the Five Civilized Tribes were being removed from the southeast to Indian Territory, U.S. settlers in northern Mexico were waging a war that culminated in 1837 with the Mexican government accepting the loss of part of its land and recognizing the newly created independent nation of Texas. Many citizens believed in the manifest destiny of the United States to extend its territorial reach from the Atlantic to the Pacific. While the Five Civilized Tribes located on land just north of Texas organized their governments, the U.S. settlers controlling the nation of Texas formed a government and debated whether or not they should remain independent or allow themselves to be annexed by the United States.

The idea of manifest destiny contained sentiments of superiority that would haunt the relationships between "Anglos" and Mexican Americans. In the minds of some white citizens, the United States was destined to rule the continent because of its Protestant culture and republican form of government. In the minds of these citizens, Mexico stood for Catholicism and feudalism. In addition, the Mexican peoples were of Spanish and Indian descent. Many of the Northern European people who settled the United States looked with scorn on the people of Spain and also wanted to rid the continent of Indian cultures.

The attitude of racial, religious, and cultural superiority—which provided motivation for the United States to take over Mexican land

and fueled hostilities between the two countries throughout the nineteenth and early twentieth centuries—was reflected in the treatment both of the Mexicans who remained after the U.S. conquest and of later Mexican immigrants. Segregated schools, housing, and discrimination in employment became the Mexican-American heritage. Reflecting the attitude of the Mexican government toward the anti-Mexican feelings in the United States, the president of Mexico, General Porfirio Díaz, was reported to have remarked in the latter part of the nineteenth century: "Poor Mexico! So far from God and so close to the United States."[13]

The evolution of discriminatory attitudes and practices toward Mexican Americans occurred in two stages. The first stage involved the treatment of the Mexicans who remained after conquest. The second stage occurred in the late nineteenth and early twentieth centuries, when U.S. farmers encouraged the immigration of farm laborers from Mexico, and political and economic conditions in Mexico caused many Mexicans to seek residence in the United States.

In *Anglos and Mexicans in the Making of Texas, 1836–1986*, David Montejano argues that a victor has the choice of either eradicating the conquered population or assimilating them to its own culture.[14] Both things occurred after the United States completed its conquest of Mexican territory. After the Texas government agreed in 1849 to be annexed to the United States, President James Polk sent a small army to the Rio Grande under the leadership of General Zachary Taylor to protect the Texas border. Taylor's presence sparked a military reaction by Mexico that resulted in the U.S. Congress declaring war on May 13, 1846. Later in the century, former President Ulysses S. Grant wrote about the declaration of war and the subsequent military campaigns as "the most unjust war ever waged by a stronger against a weaker nation . . . an instance of a republic following the bad example of European monarchies."[15]

The United States did not confine its military actions to Texas. Within one month after the congressional declaration of war, President Polk ordered a war party under the command of Colonel Stephen Kearny to travel from Fort Leavenworth, Kansas, and occupy the Mexican city of Santa Fe, New Mexico. After entering Mexican territory, Kearny issued a proclamation that "The undersigned enters New Mexico with a large military force for the purpose of seeking union with, and ameliorating the condition of the inhabitants."[16] Kearny promised, without authorization from President

Polk, that all Mexican citizens in New Mexico would be given U.S. citizenship, and he convinced many local officials to take an oath of allegiance to the U.S. government. The Mexican governor fled Santa Fe, and Kearny entered the city on August 17, 1846, without encountering any significant resistance.

One month later, on September 25, 1846, Kearny left Santa Fe for the Mexican province of California. A year before Kearny's departure from Santa Fe, a small military force under the command of Captain John C. Fremont had arrived at Fort Sutter, California. Aided by the presence of Fremont's force, a group of American settlers declared—similarly to events that occurred in Texas on July 4, 1846—that California was the Bear Flag Republic. The leaders of the new nation created a flag featuring a single star and a crude grizzly. At the celebration for the new republic, Fremont announced that he planned to conquer all of California. Military historian General John Eisenhower writes regarding Fremont's proclamation: "This pronouncement was remarkable because it was made at a time when Fremont had no knowledge of whether or not Mexico and the United States were at war."[17] On December 12, 1846, Kearny arrived in San Diego to complete the final conquest of California.

The expanding war eventually led to the occupation of Mexico City by U.S. military forces on September 14, 1847. The war ended on May 30, 1848, when the Mexican congress ratified the Treaty of Guadalupe Hidalgo, which ceded to the United States Mexican territory from Texas to California. One of the important provisions of the treaty was that all Mexican citizens remaining in the conquered territories would be granted U.S. citizenship.

Besides creating a lasting resentment toward and suspicion of the U.S. government by the Mexican government, the acquisition of Mexican lands presented the problem of what to do with the conquered Mexican citizens. The bestowal of U.S. citizenship on former Mexican citizens did not resolve the problem of the negative feelings of Anglos toward those who could not be called Mexican Americans.

As I previously mentioned, David Montejano identified two patterns in the treatment of the conquered Mexican Americans in Texas in the nineteenth century. The pattern of extermination and ejection occurred in central and southeastern Texas with the uprooting of entire communities. Mexican Americans were physically driven out of Austin in 1853 and 1855 and out of the counties of

Matagorda and Colorado in 1856. A large part of the Mexican population of San Antonio was driven out by 1856.[18]

The ejection of the Mexican population was justified by racist attitudes. Frederick Law Olmsted recorded many of these attitudes while traveling through Texas in 1855 and 1856 as a reporter for *The New York Times*. Olmsted overheard newly arrived settlers complaining that Mexicans "think themselves as good as white men" and that they were "vermin to be exterminated."[19] He found a general feeling among Anglo settlers that "white folks and Mexicans" were never meant to live together. He quoted a newspaper article published in Matagorda county that began: "The people of Matagorda county have held a meeting and ordered every Mexican to leave the county."[20] The article went on to justify the expulsion by calling the Mexicans in the area "lower class" and contending that the Mexicans were likely to take black women as wives and steal horses.

One of the important consequences of this negative action against Mexicans was to make it easier for American settlers to gain land in the area. In this case, racism served as a justification for economic exploitation. While the Mexican population declined in these areas after the war, it rose again during the early twentieth century. The same racist arguments were then used to justify paying Mexican farm workers lower wages and establishing a segregated system of schooling.

In the southern part of Texas, a different pattern developed for the treatment of the conquered Mexican population. Montejano calls this pattern a peace structure that involved two major components. One component involved bringing the Mexicans under the authority of Anglos in political matters, while the other involved an accommodation between the Mexican and Anglo elites.[21] This accommodation served as a basis for the creation of large cattle ranches. Anglo cattle raisers gained access to large tracts of land either by marrying into elite Mexican families or through direct purchase. In this accommodation, Anglos made a distinction between what they identified as the Castilian elite, who controlled vast amounts of land, and the average Mexican, who was identified as a peon. In the minds of Anglos, this division involved a racial distinction. Peons, as compared with the Castilian elite, were considered racially inferior because of their Indian ancestry. The Castilian elite were accepted because of their supposed lack of Indian heritage and Spanish ancestry. In other words, Anglos held the same racist attitudes toward peons as they did toward Indians.[22]

These racist attitudes permeated the life of the cattle ranches established in southern Texas during what is referred to as the "cowboy era" in Texas history. By the 1860s, the railroad was extended to Kansas. This made it possible to raise cattle in Texas, drive them on foot to Kansas, and then ship them east. Between 1866 and 1880 more than 4 million cattle were marched north out of Texas. The term "cowboy" was coined to describe the workers who took the herds north. The cattle drives would follow either the Chisholm Trail or the Western Trail north from southern Texas through Indian Territory to Kansas.[23] The taxes levied on the drives by the Choctaws in Indian Territory helped to support their school system.

On the cattle ranches of the cowboy era, the authority structure created a division between Mexican and Anglo cowboys. The Anglo cowboys, of course, exercised authority over the Mexican ones. In addition, facilities were segregated. Anglo cowboys ate in the ranch dining room and refused to eat with the Mexicans; Mexican cowboys camped with the herds and consumed their rations at their campsites.[24] This segregation established a pattern for later forms of segregation.

Similar to the treatment of the Indians, a major concern of the conquered Mexican population was the mandate that English was to be spoken in the schools. In 1856, two years after the Texas legislature established public schools, a law was passed requiring the teaching of English as a subject. In 1870, at the height of the cowboy era, the Texas legislature passed a school law requiring English to be the language of instruction in all public schools.[25] The same attempt to eradicate Spanish occurred in the conquered territory of California. The California Bureau of Instruction mandated in 1855 that all school classes be conducted in English. In *The Decline of the Californios: A Social History of the Spanish-Speaking California 1846–1890*, Leonard Pitt writes about the English-only requirement in public schools: "This linguistic purism went hand in hand with the nativist sentiments expressed in that year's legislature, including the suspension of the publication of state laws in Spanish."[26]

In general, Mexican Americans in the last half of the nineteenth century tried to escape the anti-Mexican attitudes of public school authorities by attending either Catholic schools or nonsectarian private schools. In California, some members of the Mexican community were interested in providing a bilingual education for their children. They wanted their children to improve their ability to read and write Spanish and become acquainted with the cultural traditions of Mexico and Spain, while at the same time learning to speak English. In some places, such as Santa Barbara, California, local Mexican leaders were able to bypass the state requirement on teaching in English and were able to maintain a bilingual public school. But in most places, bilingual instruction could be had only through schools operated by the Catholic church.[27]

In Texas, a bilingual education could be had in parochial schools and, in south Texas, in private schools established by the Mexican community. These private Mexican schools tried to maintain both the Spanish language and Mexican culture. The three major purposes of these Mexican schools were to impart Mexican ideals, teach Mexican traditions and history, and maintain racial pride among the students.[28] Because of the language issue, Mexican-American students were discouraged by local school authorities from attending the first public school opened in El Paso in 1883. Consequently, Mexican Americans opened their own Mexican Preparatory School in 1887. Similar to California, some Texas communities did not enforce the English-only rule. The first public school opened in Brownsville in 1875 was attended primarily by Mexican-American children. Since most of these children did not speak or understand English, the English-only rule was not enforced until the fourth grade.[29]

The patterns of discrimination and segregation established in the nineteenth century were accentuated during the great immigration of Mexicans into the United States during the early twentieth century. Between 1900 and 1909, 23,991 Mexicans immigrated to the United States. Between 1910 and 1919 this figure increased dramatically to 173,663, and between 1920 and 1929 the number rose to 487,775.[30]

One of the keys to understanding the continuing patterns of racism and segregation is the fact that the immigration of Mexicans was encouraged by U.S. farmers because Mexicans were an inexpensive source of labor in the booming agricultural regions of Texas and California. By the 1890s, the era of the cowboy was drawing to a close. Railroads had penetrated Texas, making the cattle drives across Indian Territory unnecessary. In addition, because of a variety of economic changes, the cattle industry itself was in a decline. Consequently, many Texans turned to farming. As the twentieth century unfolded, the expansion of the railroad made it possible to ship agricultural goods from California to the East. Similar to Texans, California farmers needed cheap labor. For some farmers, Mexicans were ideal laborers. As one Texas cotton grower put it: "They are docile and law-biding. They are the sweetest people in this position that I ever saw."[31]

Anglo attitudes about the education of the children of immigrant Mexicans involved two conflicting positions. On the one hand, farmers did not want Mexican children to go to school because school attendance meant that they were not available for farm work. On the other hand, many public officials wanted Mexican children in school so that they could be "Americanized." In addition, many Mexican families were reluctant to send their children to school because of the loss of the children's contribution to the family income.

These conflicting positions represent the two methods by which education can be used as a method of social control. One is to deny a population the knowledge necessary to protect its political and economic rights and to economically advance in society. Farmers wanted to keep Mexican laborers ignorant as a means of assuring a continued inexpensive source of labor. As one Texas farmer stated, "Educating the Mexicans is educating them away from the job, away from the dirt." Reflecting the values of the farmers in his district, one Texas school superintendent explained, "You have doubtless heard that ignorance is bliss; it seems that is so when one has to transplant onions. . . . So you see it is up to the white population to keep the Mexican on his knees in an onion patch or in new ground. This does not mix very well with education."[32] A school principal in Colorado stated, "never try to enforce compulsory attendance laws on the Mexicans. . . . The banks and the company will swear that the labor is needed and that the families need the money."[33]

Therefore, according to Guadalupe San Miguel, Jr. in *"Let All of Them Take Heed": Mexican Americans and the Campaign for Educational Equality in Texas, 1910–1981*, one of the most discriminatory acts against the children of Mexicans was the nonenforcement of compulsory school laws.[34] A survey of one Texas county in 1921 found only 30.7 percent of Mexican school-age children in school. In another Texas county in the 1920s, school authorities admitted that they enforced school attendance on Anglo children, but not on Mexican children. San Miguel, Jr. quotes one school authority from this period: "The whites come all right except one whose parents don't appreciate education. We don't enforce the attendance on the whites because we would have to on the Mexicans."[35] One school superintendent explained that he always asked the local school board if they wanted the Mexican children in school. Any enforcement of the compulsory education law against the wishes of the school board, he admitted, would probably cost him his job.[36]

Those Mexican children who did attend school faced segregation and an education designed, in a manner similar to the programs applied to Indians, to rid them of their native language and customs. School segregation for Mexican children spread rapidly throughout Texas and California. The typical pattern was for a community with a large Mexican school population to erect a separate school for Mexican children. For instance, in 1891 the Corpus Christi, Texas, school board denied admission of Mexican children to their "Anglo schools" and built a separate school.

In *Chicano Education in the Era of Segregation*, Gilbert Gonzalez finds that the typical attitude in California schools was reflected in the April 1921 minutes of the Ontario, California, Board of Education: "Mr. Hill made the recommendation that the board select two new school sites; one in the southeastern part of the town for a Mexican school; the other near the Central School."[37] Gonzalez reports that a survey conducted in the mid-1930s found that 85 percent of the districts investigated in the Southwest were segregated.[38] In *All Deliberate Speed: Segregation and Exclusion in California Schools, 1855–1975*, Charles Wollenberg quotes a California educator writing in 1920: "One of the first demands made from a community in which there is a large Mexican population is for a separate school."[39] A Los Angeles school official admitted that pressure from white citizens resulted in certain neighborhood schools being built to contain the majority of Mexican students.[40]

Besides outright racist attitudes toward Mexican Americans, school segregation was justified by the same argument used to justify isolating southeastern Indians in Indian Territory. Educators argued that the segregation of Mexican children would provide the opportunity to, in Gonzalez's words, "Americanize the child in a controlled linguistic and cultural environment, and . . . to train Mexicans for occupations considered open to, and appropriate for, them."[41]

Segregation also served the purpose, according the Montejano, of maintaining white supremacy. Anglo and Mexican children both knew that segregation was intended to separate the superior from the inferior. In addition, Mexican schools were in poorer physical condition, the Mexican children used books discarded by Anglo schools, and Mexican teams could not participate in Anglo athletic leagues. The sense of inferiority learned in the segregated educational system was reinforced in adult life by the refusal of Anglo restaurants to serve Mexicans and segregated housing.[42]

Those Mexican children attending segregated schools were put through a deculturalization program. Similar to that for the Indians who were isolated in Indian Territory and boarding schools, the deculturalization program was designed to strip away Mexican values and culture and replace the use of Spanish with English. The term most frequently used in the early twentieth century for the process of deculturalization was "Americanization." The Americanization process for Mexicans should not be confused with the Americanization programs encountered in schools by children of European immigrants. As Gilbert Gonzalez argues, the Americanization of Mexicans, as opposed to Europeans, took place in segregated school systems. In addition, the assimilation of Mexicans was made difficult by the nature of the rural economy, which locked Mexicans into segregated farm work. Anglos also showed greater disdain for Mexican culture than they did for European cultures.[43]

An important element in the Americanization of Mexican schoolchildren, as it was for Indians, was eliminating the speaking of their native language. Educators argued that learning English was essential to assimilation and the creation of a unified nation. In addition, language was considered related to values and culture. Changing languages, it was assumed, would cause a cultural revolution among Mexican Americans. Typical of this attitude was a Texas school superintendent, who was quoted by Gonzalez as saying that "a Mexican child 'is foreign in his thinking and attitudes' until he learns to 'think and talk in English.' "[44]

In 1918, Texas passed legislation with stricter requirements for the use of English in public schools. The legislation made it a criminal offense to use any language but English in the schools. In addition, the legislation required that all school personnel, including teachers, principals, custodians, and school board members, use only English when conducting school business.[45]

Similar to their attitudes regarding Indian culture and values, many Anglos believed that Mexican culture and values discouraged the exercise of economic entrepreneurship and cooperation required in an advanced corporate society. As I discussed in the previous section, it was believed by many whites that the communal lifestyle of Indians hindered their advancement in U.S. society. On the other hand, Mexicans were criticized as having a fatalistic acceptance of the human condition, being self-pitying, and being unable to work with others in large organizations. Also, many Anglos felt that Mexicans were too attached to their families and to small organizations such as local clubs.[46]

The attempted deculturalization of Mexicans did not always extend to superficial cultural aspects such as food, music, and dance. Those advocating cultural democracy felt that these cultural traditions could be maintained while attempts were made to socialize Mexican children into an entrepreneurial spirit, or what was called an "achievement concept."[47]

It is again important to stress that most Mexican children did not encounter these deculturalization programs simply because of a combination of lack of enforcement of compulsory education laws and the necessity for children to help support their families. In addition, there were reports of Mexican children dropping out of school because of the anti-Mexican bias of the curriculum. This was particularly true in Texas, where in history instruction stress was placed on the Texas defeat of Mexico.[48]

In addition, many children of migrant farm workers received little opportunity to attend school. In fact, in some areas of California, state laws on school attendance were routinely violated by local school boards to ensure the availability of children for farm work. In 1928, with support from the state, the Fresno County, California, superintendent of school opened a special migratory school. Children attended between 7:30 A.M. and 12:30 P.M. and then joined their parents in the fields. This five-hour school day was in clear violation of state law on the number of hours of attendance, but the California government never enforced this requirement on the migratory schools, and the five-hour day became typical for schools serving migrant children. In some parts of California, migrant children were completely denied an education. In the 1930s, public schools in Ventura County, California, displayed signs reading "No Migratory Children Wanted Here."[49]

Of course, many in the Mexican-American community

protested against this denial of education to their children, the existence of school segregation, and the attempts at deculturalization. In 1929, representatives from a variety of Mexican-American organizations met in Corpus Christi, Texas, to form the League of United Latin American Citizens (LULAC). This organization was primarily composed of middle-class Mexican Americans, as opposed to Mexican farm laborers and migratory workers. In fact, membership was restricted to U.S. citizens.[50]

LULAC adopted a code that reflected the desire of middle-class Mexican Americans to integrate the culture of Mexico with that of the United States. The code attempted to balance a respect for U.S. citizenship with a maintenance of cultural traditions. On the one hand, the code asked members to "Respect your citizenship, converse it; honor your country, maintain its traditions in the minds of your children, incorporate yourself in the culture and civilization." On the other hand, the code told its members to "Love the men of your race, take pride in your origins and keep it immaculate; respect your glorious past and help to vindicate your people."[51]

Clearly, LULAC was committed to a vision of the United States that was multicultural and multilingual. In contrast to the public schools, which were trying to eradicate Mexican culture and the use of Spanish, LULAC favored bilingualism and instruction in the cultural traditions of the United States and Mexico. The LULAC code called upon its members to "Study the past of your people, or the country to which you owe your citizenship; learn to handle with purity the two most essential languages, English and Spanish."[52]

As an organization, LULAC was dedicated to fighting discrimination against Mexican Americans, particularly in the form of school segregation. In fact, one of the founders of LULAC, J. Luz Saenz, argued that discrimination and the lack of equal educational opportunities were hindering integration of Mexicans into U.S. society. In summarizing the position of LULAC, Saenz stated, "As long as they do not educate us with all the guarantees and opportunities for free participation in all . . . activities . . . as long as they wish to raise up on high the standard of SUPREMACY OF RACES ON ACCOUNT OF COLOR. . . so much will they put off our conversion . . . [to] full citizens."[53]

LULAC's first challenge to school segregation occurred in 1928 with the filing of a complaint against the Charlotte, Texas, Independent School District. In this case, a child of unknown racial background adopted by a Mexican family was refused admission to the local Anglo elementary school and was assigned to the Mexican school. Her father argued that because of her unknown racial background, she should be put into the Anglo school. The state admitted that the local school district did not have the right to segregate Mexican children. On the other hand, local school officials justified the segregation of Mexican children because they required special instruction in English. After determining that the child spoke fluent English, the state school superintendent ordered the local school district to enroll the student in the Anglo school. While this potentially opened the doors of Anglo schools to Mexican children who spoke fluent English, it did little to end segregation.[54]

LULAC's second case involving school segregation occurred in 1930 when the Del Rio, Texas, Independent School District proposed a bond election to construct and improve school buildings. Included in the proposal were improvements for the Mexican school. Mexican-American parents in the district complained that the proposal continued the practice of segregating their children from other students. The local superintendent defended segregation as necessary because Mexican students had irregular attendance records and special language problems. The court accepted the arguments of local school authorities that segregation was necessary for educational reasons. On the other hand, the court did state that it was unconstitutional to segregate students on the basis of national origin. This decision presented LULAC with the difficult problem of countering the educational justifications used for segregation. At a special 1931 session, LULAC members called for scientific studies of arguments that segregation is necessary for instruction.[55]

While LULAC focused most of its efforts on school segregation, there was a concern about what was perceived to be the anti-Mexican bias of textbooks. In 1939, the state president of LULAC, Ezequiel Salinas, attacked the racism and distortions of Mexicans in history textbooks. Significant changes in the racial content of textbooks did not, however, occur until the full impact of the civil rights movement hit the publishing industry in the 1960s.[56]

While LULAC was struggling to end segregation in Texas, Mexican-American organizations in California were attacking the same problem. By the 1930s, Mexican children were the most segregated group in the state. The California situation was somewhat different from that of Texas, because of a 1935 state law allowing for the segregation of Chinese, Japanese, "Mongolians," and Indians. While Indians born in the United States were exempt from this law, the state did allow segregation of "descendants of the original American Indians of the United States." According to Charles Wollenberg, "In this torturous and indirect fashion, the 1935 law seemed to allow for segregation of Mexican 'Indians,' but not of Mexican 'whites.' "[57]

The struggle to end segregation played a major role in the great civil rights movement of the post-World War II period. The efforts of both the NAACP and LULAC finally resulted in the end of legal segregation of African-American and Mexican-American students. While the great civil rights movement brought the end of segregation, it also opened the door to feelings of racial and cultural pride. From World War II to the 1990s, Native Americans, Puerto Ricans, African Americans, and Mexican Americans have demanded that public schools recognize their distinct cultures and incorporate these cultures into curricula and textbooks.

NOTES

1. Ronald Takaki, *Strangers From a Different Shore: A History of Asian Americans* (New York: Penguin Books, 1989), pp. 203–205.
2. Ronald Takaki, *A Different Mirror: A History of Multicultural America* (Boston: Little, Brown and Company, 1993), p. 207.
3. Takaki, *Strangers From a Different Shore*, p. 299.
4. Ibid., p. 299.
5. Takaki, *A Different Mirror*, pp. 191–225.
6. Quoted in Ibid., p. 205.
7. Victor Low, *The Unimpressible Race: A Century of Educational Struggle by the Chinese in San Francisco* (San Francisco: East/West Publishing, 1982), p. 48.
8. Ibid., p. 61.
9. Ibid., p. 62.
10. Ibid., p. 67.
11. Charles M. Wollenberg, *All Deliberate Speed: Segregation and Exclusion in California Schools, 1855–1975* (Berkeley: University of California Press, 1976), p. 53.
12. Ibid., pp. 53–60.
13. Quoted in John S. D. Eisenhower, *So Far from God: The U.S. War with Mexico 1846–1848* (New York: Anchor Books, 1989), p. xv.
14. David Montejano, *Anglos and Mexicans in the Making of Texas, 1836–1986* (Austin: University of Texas Press, 1987), p. 25.

15. Eisenhower, *So Far from God*, p. xvii.
16. Ibid., p. 208.
17. Ibid., p. 214.
18. Montejano, *Anglos and Mexicans*, pp. 28–29.
19. Ibid., p. 29.
20. Ibid., p. 28.
21. Ibid., p. 34.
22. Ibid., p. 84.
23. Ibid., pp. 53–56.
24. Ibid., pp. 83–84.
25. Guadalupe San Miguel, Jr., *"Let All of Them Take Heed": Mexican Americans and the Campaign for Educational Equality in Texas, 1910–1981* (Austin: University of Texas Press, 1987), pp. 6–7.
26. Leonard Pitt, *The Decline of the Californios: A Social History of the Spanish-Speaking California 1846–1890* (Berkeley: University of California Press, 1968), p. 226.
27. Ibid., pp. 225–226.
28. San Miguel, *"Let All of Them Take Heed,"* p. 10.
29. Ibid., p. 11.
30. Montejano, *Anglos and Mexicans*, p. 180.
31. Quoted in Ibid., p. 188.
32. Quoted in Ibid., p. 193.
33. Gilbert Gonzalez, *Chicano Education in the Era of Segregation* (Philadelphia: Balch Institute Press, 1990), p. 108.
34. San Miguel, *"Let All of Them Take Heed,"* p. 47.
35. Ibid., pp. 48–49.
36. Ibid., p. 50.
37. Gonzalez, *Chicano Education*, p. 21.
38. Ibid., p. 22.
39. Charles M. Wollenberg, *All Deliberate Speed*, p. 111.
40. Ibid., p. 112.
41. Ibid., p. 22.
42. Montejano, *Anglos and Mexicans*, pp. 230–231.
43. Gonzalez, *Chicano Education*, pp. 35–36.
44. Ibid., p. 41.
45. San Miguel, *"Let All of Them Take Heed,"* p. 33.
46. Gonzalez, *Chicano Education*, pp. 133–134.
47. Ibid., pp. 134–135.
48. Montejano, *Anglos and Mexicans*, p. 231.
49. Gonzalez, *Chicano Education*, p. 105.
50. Mario T. Garcia, *Mexican Americans: Leadership, Ideology, and Identity 1930–1960* (New Haven: Yale University Press, 1989), pp. 25–62.
51. Ibid., p. 30.

52. Ibid.
53. Quoted in San Miguel, *"Let All of Them Take Heed,"* p. 72.
54. Ibid., pp. 76–78.
55. Ibid., pp. 79–80.
56. For a study of changes in the racial composition of textbooks, see Joel Spring, *Images of American Life: A History of Ideological Management in Schools, Movies, Radio, and Television* (Albany: State University of New York Press, 1992), pp. 205–214.
57. Wollenberg, *All Deliberate Speed*, p. 118.

CHAPTER 6

The Great Civil Rights Movement and the New Culture Wars

Extending from the 1940s into the 1990s, the great civil rights movement was a continuation of the culture wars initiated by English colonists when they invaded Native American lands in North America. From the time of the invasion to the 1990s, many citizens tried to assure that Protestant Anglo-American culture would be the dominant culture of the United States. For instance, in the 1990s, historian Arthur Schlesinger, who opposed multicultural education in public schools and advocated the teaching of Protestant Anglo-American culture, wrote, "For better or worse, the white Anglo-Saxon Protestant tradition was for two centuries—and in crucial respects still is—the dominant influence on American culture and society."[1]

In the nineteenth and twentieth centuries, those believing the United States should be united by a Protestant Anglo-American culture advocated the "civilization" and deculturalization of Native Americans, Mexican Americans, Puerto Ricans, and Jewish and Catholic immigrants from southern and eastern Europe. Some citizens believed in the racial superiority of whites that resulted in the segregation of African Americans, Native Americans, Mexican Americans, and Asian Americans. In the early twentieth century, believers in the racial superiority of whites, particularly whites from England and Germany, used standardized testing to provide validity to their views.

The great civil rights movement was composed of dominated groups who protested the domination of Protestant Anglo-American culture. Activists among Native Americans, African Americans, Mexican Americans, Asian Americans, and Puerto Ricans demanded restoration and recognition of their cultures. Many of these activists rejected the idea of a single dominating culture for the idea of a pluralistic society with many cultures given recognition in the public schools. Besides demands for cultural pluralism, activists demanded the end of school segregation and racism in educational practices.

Leading the way in the great civil rights movement were members of the National Association for the Advancement of Colored People (NAACP), who fought the continuation of segregation in schools and public facilities, and the lack of opportunity to participate in the American economic system. In addition, they demanded recognition for African-American culture in the public schools. The actions of African Americans contributed to the militancy of other groups in demanding equality of educational opportunity and recognition of their cultures in public schools.

Native Americans campaigned for self-determination and cultural recognition. Mexican Americans continued their struggles against segregation and they sought preservation of Mexican culture and the Spanish language in the schools. By the 1960s, Puerto Ricans joined Mexican Americans in supporting bilingual education.

Also, the great civil rights movement opened the door to demands that the public schools reflect minority cultures. African Americans, Native Americans, Mexican Americans, Asian Americans, and Puerto Ricans demanded that their unique cultures be recognized and be given a place in the school curriculum. These demands gave impetus to the movement for multicultural education in the 1980s and 1990s.

SCHOOL DESEGREGATION

The desegregation of American schools was the result of over a half century of struggle by the black community. Since its founding in the early part of the twentieth century, the NAACP had struggled to end discriminatory practices against minority groups. The school desegregation issue was finally decided by the U.S. Supreme Court in 1954 in *Brown* v. *Board of Education of Topeka*. The decision did not bring immediate results, because resistance to court-ordered desegregation arose. The frustration caused by the slow pace of school integration and the continuation of other forms of discrimination contributed to the growth of a massive civil rights movement in the late 1950s and early 1960s. The response of national political leaders to the civil rights movement was the enactment of strong civil rights legislation.

It is important to remember that school desegregation and civil rights legislation were not the products of a benign government but were the result of tremendous struggle and public demonstrations. Politically, African Americans were forced by their lack of power at local and state levels to seek redress for their grievances from the federal government. National leaders tried to avoid dealing with civil rights issues but were finally forced by public demonstrations to take action. With regard to schooling, federal action resulted in greater federal control of local schools and a feeling among school board members that local control of education was rapidly disappearing.

The key legal issue in the struggle for desegregation was the interpretation of the Fourteenth Amendment to the Constitution. This constitutional amendment was ratified in 1868, shortly after the close of the Civil War. One of its purposes was to extend the basic guarantees of the Bill of Rights into the areas under state and local government control. The most important and controversial section of the Fourteenth Amendment states, "No State shall make or enforce any law which shall abridge the privileges or immunities of citizens . . . nor . . . deprive any person of life, liberty, or property, without due process of law; nor deny to any person within its jurisdiction the equal protection of the laws."

A major test of the meaning of the Fourteenth Amendment with regard to segregation occurred in 1895 in a Supreme Court case involving Homer Plessy, who was one-eighth black and seven-eighths white and had been arrested for refusing to ride in the "colored" coach of a train, as required by Louisiana law. The Supreme Court ruled that segregation did not create a badge of inferiority if segregated facilities were equal and the law was reasonable. In establishing the "separate but equal doctrine," the Supreme Court failed to clearly define what constitutes equal facilities and what is reasonable.

The overturning of the separate but equal doctrine and a broader application of the Fourteenth Amendment came in 1954 in the historic and controversial Supreme Court decision *Brown* v. *Board of Education of Topeka*. In 1953, *Brown* was one of the five school segregation suits to reach the Supreme Court. It became the first case simply because the five cases were heard in alphabetical order. The Brown case began in 1951, when Oliver Brown and twelve other parents represented by NAACP lawyers brought suit to void a Kansas law that permitted but did not require local segregation of the schools. In this particular case, Oliver Brown's daughter was denied the right to attend a white elementary school within five blocks of her home and forced to cross railroad tracks and travel twenty-one blocks to attend an all-black school. The federal district court in Kansas ruled against Oliver Brown, using the argument that the segregated schools named in the suit were substantially equal and thus fell within the separate but equal doctrine.

In preparing its brief for the Supreme Court, the NAACP defined two important objectives: (1) to show that the climate of the times required an end to segregation laws and (2) to show that the separate but equal doctrine contained a contradiction in terms—that is, that separate facilities were inherently unequal. Evidence from recent findings in the social sciences presented by the NAACP to prove that separate facilities were inherently unequal provided the basis for overturning the separate but equal doctrine. It also caused a storm of protest alleging that the Supreme Court was basing decisions on nonlegal arguments. Throughout the South, it was widely believed that the Court was being persuaded by communist-oriented social scientists. Billboards appeared on highways demanding the impeachment of Chief Justice Earl Warren for his role in subverting the Constitution.

The Supreme Court argued in the Brown decision, "In the field of public education the doctrine of 'separate but equal' has no place. Separate educational facilities are inherently unequal." To support this argument, the Supreme Court wrote one of the most controversial single sentences ever to appear in a Court decision: "Whatever may have been the extent of psychological knowledge at the time of *Plessy* v. *Ferguson* this finding is amply supported by modern authority."[2]

In 1955 the Supreme Court issued its enforcement decree for the desegregation of schools. One problem facing the Court was the lack of machinery for supervising and ensuring the desegregation of vast numbers of segregated school districts. The Court resolved this problem by relying on federal district courts to determine the equitable principles for desegregation. Federal judges were often part of the social fabric of their local communities and resisted attempts at speedy desegregation. Consequently, integration occurred at a slow pace until additional civil rights legislation was passed in the 1960s and the mounting frustrations in the black community fed the flames of a militant civil rights movement.[4]

The evolution of the mass media in the 1950s was an important factor in the civil rights movement because it became possible to turn local problems into national issues. Thus, even though presidents had traditionally shown a great deal of deference to the important white southern political structure, the emergence of the mass media as a powerful force allowed both the federal government and civil rights groups to put unprecedented pressure on southern political leaders, forcing them to comply with national civil rights legislation. In fact, enforcement of the Supreme Court school desegregation ruling depended in large part on civil rights groups making effective use of television. In one sense, the struggle that took place was a struggle between public images. Concern over America's international image grew as pictures of racial injustice flashed around the world, and the president's public image was often threatened when examples of racial injustice were shown to millions of television viewers and the question was asked, What is our president doing about this situation?

The most dramatic technique used by civil rights groups was nonviolent confrontation. The massive nonviolent response of black people in the South confronted with an array of cattle prods, clubs, and fire hoses wielded by cursing southern law enforcement units provided dramatic and shocking television viewing for the nation. The Congress on Racial Equality (CORE), the Student Nonviolent Coordinating Committee (SNCC), and the Southern Christian Leadership Conference (SCLC), led by the Reverend Martin Luther King, Jr., provided the national drama and the final push for national civil rights legislation.

The introduction of nonviolent confrontation into the civil rights movement came from the Christian student movement of the 1930s, which, under the leadership of the Fellowship for Reconciliation, was committed to use of the Gandhian technique of *satyagraha* (nonviolent direct action) in solving racial and industrial problems in the United States. CORE, a major organization in the civil rights movement, was organized at the University of Chicago in 1942. The two basic doctrines of the early CORE movement were commitment to racial integration and the use of Christian nonviolent techniques.

CORE did not rise to national prominence until the late 1950s, when another Christian leader, Dr. Martin Luther King, Jr., made nonviolent confrontation the central drama of the civil rights movement. King was born in 1929 in Atlanta, Georgia, into a family of Baptist ministers. His maternal grandfather founded the Ebenezer Baptist Church, and his father made the church into one of the largest and most prestigious Baptist churches in Atlanta. In 1944, King entered Atlanta's Morehouse College, where he claimed to have been influenced by his reading of Henry David Thoreau's *Essay on Civil Disobedience*. He later wrote about the essay, "Fascinated by the idea of refusing to cooperate with an evil system, I was so deeply moved that I reread the work several times. This was my first intellectual contact with the theory of non-violent resistance."[4]

In 1948, King entered the Crozier Theological Seminary in Chester, Pennsylvania, where for the first time he became acquainted with pacifism through a lecture by A. J. Muste. King wrote that at the time he considered Muste's pacifist doctrine impractical in a world confronted by the armies of totalitarian nations. Of more importance to King's intellectual development was his exposure to the social gospel philosophy of Walter Rauschenbusch, which actively involved the church in social reform as a means of creating a kingdom of God on earth. Although he rejected the optimistic elements in the social gospel, King argued that any concern with the souls of humans required a concern with social and economic conditions.

King also studied the lectures and works of Mohandas K. Gandhi. The Indian leader's work convinced King that the Christian doctrine of love could be a force for social change. King wrote, "Gandhi was probably the first person in history to lift the love ethic of Jesus above mere interaction between individuals to a powerful and effective social force on a large scale." Like the early members of CORE, King became convinced that nonviolent resistance "was the only morally and practically sound method open to oppressed people in their struggle for freedom."[5]

The incident that launched Martin Luther King's civil rights activities and provided scope for his Gandhian form of the social gospel occurred on December 1, 1955. On that date, Rosa Parks, who had worked a regular day as a seamstress in one of the leading department stores in Montgomery, Alabama, boarded a bus and took the first seat behind the section reserved for whites. Later during the journey home, several white passengers boarded the bus. The driver ordered Rosa Parks and three other black passengers to stand so that the white passengers could have seats. Rosa Parks refused and was arrested. The black ministers in the community quickly organized in response to this incident, and on December 5 the Montgomery bus boycott began.

The bus boycott lasted for over a year and finally ended on December 21, 1956, when, after a Supreme Court decision against segregation on buses, the Montgomery transit system was officially integrated. King emerged from the struggle a national hero among dominated groups. In 1957 he organized the Southern Christian Leadership Conference (SCLC), which became the central organization in the civil rights struggle.

After SCLC was formed, boycotts and nonviolent demonstrations began to occur throughout the South. On May 17, 1957, Martin Luther King gave his first national address in Washington, D.C. He told his audience, "Give us the ballot and we will quietly, lawfully, and nonviolently, without rancor or bitterness, implement the May 17, 1954, decision of the Supreme Court." For King, meaningful school desegregation depended on the power of the black voter.

As civil rights demonstrations increased in intensity, national leaders began to work for federal legislation. In 1957 and 1960, two ineffective forms of civil rights legislation were passed by Congress. The most important civil rights legislation was not enacted until 1964, when violence in Birmingham, Alabama, and a mass march on Washington forced a response from the federal government. The civil rights movement made Birmingham and its director of safety, Eugene "Bull" Connor, symbols of the oppression of black people in the United States. President John F. Kennedy was quoted as saying, "Our judgment of Bull Connor should not be too harsh. After all, in his way, he has done a good deal for civil rights legislation this year."[6] The March on Washington symbolized to Congress and the American people the growing strength of the civil rights movement and provided the stage for television coverage of speeches by civil rights leaders.

The result of these activities was the Civil Rights Act of 1964. Under eleven different titles, the power of federal regulations was extended in the areas of voting rights, public accommodations, education, and employment. Titles IV and VI of the legislation were intended to end school segregation and provide authority for implementing the Brown decision.

Title VI, the most important section, establishes the precedent for using disbursement of government money as a means of controlling educational policies. Originally, President Kennedy merely proposed a requirement that institutions receiving federal funds must end discriminatory practices. In its final form, Title VI required mandatory withholding of federal funds to institutions that did not comply with its mandates. It states that no person, on the basis of race, color, or national origin, can be excluded from or denied the benefits of any program receiving federal financial assistance, and it requires all federal agencies to establish guidelines to implement this policy. Refusal by institutions or projects to follow these guidelines will result in the "termination of or refusal to grant or to continue assistance under such program or activity."

The power of Title VI rests in its ability to withhold federal money from financially pressed school systems. This became a more crucial issue after the passage in 1965 of the Elementary and Secondary Education Act. The rate of desegregation was more rapid after the 1964 Civil Rights Act than before, but abundant evidence by the end of the 1960s showed that segregated education continued in the South. One political scientist argued that school desegregation in the South by 1968 looked massive compared to the level in the early 1960s, but compared to an ideal of total integration, the actual results could be labeled as token. By defining a desegregated school as one that blacks attended and where more than 20 percent of the school population was white, a sample of 894 counties in the South found that 5 percent or less of the black pupils were attending integrated schools in 25 percent of the counties and 10 percent or less in 40 percent of the counties. At a level approaching genuine integration, in 20 percent of the counties 90 percent or more of the black pupils were reported to be attending integrated schools. For all southern counties, the median attending integrated schools was 15.6 percent.[7]

School desegregation moved at an even slower pace in the North. Originally it was believed that the Brown decision would affect only those states whose laws required segregated education. However, by the late 1960s, the courts began to rule that the Brown decision applied to all schools in the country, if it could be proved that segregation was the result of intentional actions by school boards or school administrators.

NATIVE AMERICANS

As African Americans were leading the fight against segregated schooling, Native Americans were attempting to gain control of the education of their children and restore their cultural heritage and languages to the curriculum. Native Americans shared a common interest with Mexican Americans and Puerto Ricans in supporting bilingual and multicultural education.

During the 1940s and 1950s, federal Indian policy was directed at termination of tribes and reservations. The leader of the termination policy, Senator Arthur V. Watkins of Utah, declared in 1957, "I see the following words emblazoned in letters of fire above the heads of the Indians—THESE PEOPLE SHALL BE FREE!"[8] Freedom in this case meant freedom from federal supervision and control. It also meant the end of official tribal status.

Termination policies attempted to break up tribal relations by relocating Indians to urban areas. Relocation to urban areas was similar to the nineteenth-century federal policy that sent Native Americans to Indian Territory and reservations. But, in this case, Indians were to be "civilized" by being dispersed throughout the general population.

Termination efforts met stiff resistance from Indian and white civil rights activists. In 1961, 450 Indian delegates from ninety tribes attended the American Indian Chicago Conference at the University of Chicago. The delegates issued a *Declaration of Indian Purpose* calling for the end of termination policies. In the end, termination policy resulted in about 3 percent of the Indian tribes being terminated, including the Menominee of Wisconsin and the Klamath Indians of Oregon.[9]

While resisting termination policies, Native Americans began to demand greater self-determination. This was reflected in policy changes in the Bureau of Indian Affairs after the election of John F. Kennedy in 1960. Condemning the termination policies of the 1950s, the Kennedy administration advocated Indian participation in decisions regarding federal policies. Kennedy's secretary of the interior,

Stewart Udall, appointed a Task Force on Indian Affairs, which, in its 1961 report, states, "to insure the success of our endeavor we must solicit the collaboration of those whom we hope to benefit—the Indians themselves . . . equal citizenship, maximum self-sufficiency, and full participation in American life."[10]

One of the results of the drive for self-determination was the creation of the Rough Rock Demonstration School in 1966. Established on a Navajo reservation in Arizona, the school was a joint effort of the Office of Economic Opportunity and the Bureau of Indian Affairs. One of the major goals of the demonstration school was for Navajo parents to control the education of their children and participate in all aspects of their schooling.[11]

Besides tribal control, one of the important features of the Rough Rock Demonstration School was the attempt to preserve the Navajo language and culture. In contrast to the deculturalization efforts of the nineteenth and early twentieth centuries, the goal of learning both Navajo and English was presented as a means of preparing children to "fend successfully in both cultures and see the Navajo way as part of a universal system of values."[12]

The struggle for self-determination was aided by the development of a Pan-Indian movement in the United States. The Pan-Indian movement was based on the assumption that Native American tribes shared a common set of values and interests. Similar to the role played by CORE and SCLC among African Americans, Pan-Indian organizations, such as the American Indian Movement (AIM) and the Indians of All Tribes, led demonstrations demanding self-determination. In 1969, members of the Indians of All Tribes seized Alcatraz Island in San Francisco Bay as a means of calling attention to the plight of Native Americans and demanded that the island, which Indians had originally sold to the federal government for $24 worth of beads, be made an Indian cultural and education center. In 1972, AIM organized a march on Washington, D.C., called the Trail of Broken Treaties. Members of the march seized the Bureau of Indian Affairs and hung a large sign at the entrance declaring it the American Indian Embassy.[13]

INDIAN EDUCATION: A NATIONAL TRAGEDY

Throughout the 1960s and 1970s, federal administrators gave support to Indian demands for self-determination. During his election campaign in 1968, Richard M. Nixon declared, "The right of self-determination of the Indian people will be respected and their participation in planning their own destiny will actively be encouraged."[14]

It was in this climate of civil rights activism and political support for Indian self-determination that the U.S. Senate Committee on Labor and Public Welfare issued in 1969 the report *Indian Education: A National Tragedy—A National Challenge*. The report opened with a statement condemning previous educational policies of the federal government: "A careful review of the historical literature reveals that the dominant policy of the Federal Government toward the American Indian has been one of forced assimilation . . . [because of] a desire to divest the Indian of his land."[15]

After a lengthy review of the failure of past educational policies, the report's first recommendation was "maximum participation and control by Indians in establishing Indian education programs."[16] In its second recommendation, the report called for maximum Indian participation in the development of educational programs in federal schools and local public schools. These educational programs were to include early childhood education, vocational education, work-study, and adult literacy education. Of special importance was the recommendation to create bilingual and bicultural education programs.

Native American demands for bilingual and bicultural education were aided by the passage of Title VII of the Elementary and Secondary Education Act of 1968 or, as it was also called, the Bilingual Education Act. This was, as I will explain later in this chapter, a product of political activism by Mexican-American groups. Native Americans used funds provided under this legislation to support bilingual programs in Indian languages and English. For instance, the Bilingual Education Act provided support for bilingual programs in Navajo and English at the previously mentioned Rough Rock Demonstration School.[17]

The congressional debates resulting from the criticism leveled at Indian education in the report *Indian Education: A National Tragedy—A National Challenge* eventually culminated in the passage of the Indian Education Act in 1972. The declared policy of the legislation was to provide financial assistance to local schools to develop programs to meet the "special" educational needs of Native American students. In addition, the legislation created a federal Office of Indian Education.[18]

In 1974, the Bureau of Indian Affairs issued a set of procedures for protecting student rights and due process. In contrast to the brutal and dictatorial treatment of Indian students in the boarding schools of the late nineteenth and early twentieth centuries, each Indian student was extended the right "to make his or her own decisions where applicable."[19] And, in striking contrast to earlier deculturalization policies, Indian students were granted "the right to freedom of religion and culture."[20]

The most important piece of legislation supporting self-determination was the 1975 Indian Self-Determination and Education Assistance Act, which gave tribes the power to contract with the federal government to run their own education and health programs. The legislation opened with the declaration that it was "An Act to provide maximum Indian participation in the Government and education of Indian people; to provide for the full participation of Indian tribes in programs and services conducted by the federal government."[21]

The Indian Self-Determination and Education Assistance Act strengthened Indian participation in the control of education programs. The legislation provided that, in a local school district receiving funds for the education of Indian students that did not have a school board having a majority of Indians, the district had to establish a separate local committee composed of parents of Indian students in the school. This committee was given the authority over any Indian education programs contracted with the federal government.

The principles embodied in the Indian Self-Determination and Education Assistance Act were expanded upon in 1988 with the passage of the Tribally Controlled Schools Act. In addition to the right to operate schools under federal contract as provided in the 1975 legislation, the Tribally Controlled Schools Act provided for outright grants to tribes to support the operation of their own schools.[22]

Efforts to protect Indian culture was strengthened with the passage in 1978 of a congressional resolution on American Indian religious freedom. Remember that missionaries and federal policies from the seventeenth to the early twentieth centuries attempted to eradicate Indian religions and replace them with Christianity. The resolution recognized these earlier attempts to abridge Indian rights to religious freedom, stating: "That henceforth it shall be the policy of the United States to protect and preserve for American Indians their inherent right of freedom to believe, express and exercise traditional religions . . . and the freedom to worship through ceremonial and traditional rites."[23]

In addition to the protection of religion, the federal government committed itself to promoting traditional languages with the passage of the Native American Languages Act of 1990. This act commits the federal government to "preserve, protect, and promote the rights and freedom of Native Americans to use, practice, and develop Native American languages."[24]

There is, of course, an ironic twist to federal legislation designed to promote self-determination and preservation of Native American languages, religions, and cultures when placed against the backdrop of history. The Five Civilized Tribes in Indian Territory were operating their own tribal governments and school systems in the nineteenth century. The Cherokees were conducting bilingual education programs and protecting their cultural and religious traditions. These forms of self-determination and protection of languages and cultures ended when Indian Territory was dissolved in 1907. Also, the tribes placed onto reservations in the nineteenth century were subjected to policies consciously designed to destroy their cultures, languages, and religions. Therefore, the federal legislation of the 1970s and 1980s, which were designed to reserve these policies, required many tribes to discover and resurrect languages and traditions that the federal government had already partially destroyed.

MEXICAN AMERICANS

Similar to African Americans, Mexican Americans turned to the courts to seek redress for their grievances. In Ontario, California, in 1945, Mexican-American parents demanded that the school board grant all requests for transfer out of the Mexican schools. When the board refused this request, Gonzalo Mendez and William Guzman brought suit for violation of the Fourteenth Amendment to the Constitution. The school board responded to this suit by claiming that segregation was not based on race or national origins but on the necessity of providing special instruction.[25]

In 1946 a U.S. District Court ruled in *Mendez et al.* v. *Westminster School District of Orange County* that Mexicans were not Indians as claimed under the 1935 California law. The judge argued that the only possible argument for segregation was the special educational needs of Mexican-American children. These needs centered around the issue of learning English. Completely reversing the educational justification for segregation, the judge argued that "evidence clearly shows that Spanish-speaking children are retarded in learning English by lack of exposure to its use by segregation."[26] Therefore, the court ruled that segregation was illegal because it was not required by state law and because there was no valid educational justification for segregation.[27]

Heartened by the Mendez decision, the League of United Latin American Citizens (LULAC), the Mexican-American equivalent of the NAACP, forged ahead in its legal attack on segregation in Texas. With support from LULAC, a group of parents in 1948 brought suit against the Bastrop Independent School District, charging that local school authorities had no legal right to segregate children of Mexican descent and that this segregation was solely because the children were of Mexican descent. In *Delgado* v. *Bastrop Independent School District*, the court ruled that segregating Mexican-American children was illegal and discriminatory. The ruling required that the local school district end all segregation. The court did give local school districts the right to separate some children in the first grade only if scientific tests showed that they needed special instruction in English and the separation took place on the same campus.[28]

In general, LULAC was pleased with the decision. The one point they were dissatisfied with was the provision for the separation of children in the first grade. This allowed local schools to practice what was referred to in the latter part of the twentieth century as "second-generation segregation." Second-generation segregation refers to the practice of using educational justifications for segregating children within a single school building. In fact, many local Texas school districts did use the proviso for that purpose.[29]

While the Mendez and Delgado decisions did hold out the promise of ending segregation of Mexican Americans, local school districts used many tactics to avoid integration, including manipulation of school district lines, choice plans, and different forms of second-generation segregation. For instance, the California State Department of Education reported in 1966 that 57 percent of the children with Spanish surnames were still attending schools that were predominantly Mexican American. In 1973, a civil rights activist, John Caughey, estimated that two-thirds of the Mexican-

American children in Los Angeles attended segregated schools. In *All Deliberate Speed: Segregation and Exclusion in California Schools, 1855–1975*, Charles Wollenberg estimates that in California by 1973 more Mexican and Mexican-American children attended segregated schools than in 1947.[30]

The continuation of de facto forms of segregation resulted in the formation in 1967 of the Mexican American Legal Defense and Education Fund (MALDEF). Initially, MALDEF focused on cases dealing with students who were punished for participating in civil rights activities. In 1968, MALDEF focused its attention on the inequitable funding of school districts in Texas that primarily served Mexican Americans. Not only were Mexican-American children facing de facto segregation, but the schools they were attending were also receiving less funding than schools attended by Anglos.[31]

The case brought by MALDEF, *Rodriguez* v. *San Antonio Independent School District*, had major implications for financing of schools across the country. In the case, a group of Mexican-American parents brought a class action suit against the state of Texas for the inequitable funding of school districts. In 1971, a federal district court ruled that the Texas school finance system was unconstitutional. In its decision, the federal district court applied—as the U.S. Supreme Court had in the 1954 school desegregation case—the equal protection clause of the Fourteenth Amendment. The inequality in financing of school districts was considered a denial of equal opportunity for Mexican-American children to receive an education. The U.S. Supreme Court overturned the decision on March 12, 1973, with the argument that school finance was not a constitutional issue. This Supreme Court decision meant that all school finance cases would have to be dealt with in state courts. Since 1973, numerous cases involving inequality in the financing of public schools have been argued in state courts.[32]

In 1970, Mexican Americans were officially recognized by the federal courts as an identifiable dominated group in the public schools in a MALDEF case, *Cisneros* v. *Corpus Christi Independent School District*. A central issue in the case was whether or not the 1954 school desegregation decision could be applied to Mexican Americans. The original Brown decision had dealt specifically with African Americans who were segregated by state and local laws. In his final decision, Judge Owen Cox ruled that blacks and Mexican Americans were segregated in the Corpus Christi school system law and that Mexican Americans were an identifiable dominated group because of their language, culture, religion, and Spanish surnames.[33]

BILINGUAL EDUCATION: THE CULTURE WARS CONTINUED

Since the efforts of Noah Webster in the late eighteenth and early nineteenth centuries to create a national language, Native Americans and Spanish-speaking residents were concerned about preserving their languages. In the 1960s, a new chapter in the culture wars was opened when Native Americans, Mexican Americans, and Puerto Ricans joined in efforts to have the public schools implement bilingual education programs. Those opposed to multicultural education quickly reacted to the bilingual education movement by arguing that the official language of the United States should be English.

During the 1960s, Mexican Americans began to demonstrate for the use of Spanish in schools and the teaching of Mexican-American history and culture. In 1968, Mexican-American students boycotted four East Los Angeles high schools, demanding bilingual programs, courses in Mexican-American history and culture, and the serving of Mexican food in the school cafeterias. In addition, the students demanded the hiring of more Spanish-speaking teachers and the firing of teachers who appeared to be anti-Mexican American.[34]

The school boycotts in Los Angeles attracted the attention of the newly formed La Raza Unida. La Raza Unida was formed in 1967, when a group of Mexican Americans boycotted federal hearings on the conditions of Mexican Americans and started their own conference. At the conference, La Raza Unida took a militant stand on the protection of the rights of Mexican Americans and the preservation of their culture and language. A statement drafted at the first conference proclaimed: "the time of subjugation, exploitation, and abuse of human rights of La Raza in the United States is hereby ended forever."[35]

La Raza Unida's statement on the preservation of culture and language reflected the growing mood in the Mexican-American community that public schools needed to pay more attention to dominated cultures and languages. The statement drafted at the first conference affirmed "the greatness of our heritage, our history, our language, our traditions, our contributions to humanity and our culture."[36]

Politicians responded to Mexican-American and Puerto Rican demands for the presentation of Spanish in the schools. Liberal Democratic Senator Ralph Yarborough of Texas, believing that he would lose the 1970 election to a wealthy and conservative Democrat, decided that Hispanic support was crucial to his coalition of blacks, Mexican Americans, and poor whites. In an effort to win Hispanic support, Yarborough, after being appointed to a special subcommittee on bilingual education of the Senate Committee on Labor and Public Welfare, launched a series of hearings in major Hispanic communities.[37]

The testimony at these hearings came primarily from representatives of the Mexican-American and Puerto Rican communities, not educational experts or linguistic theorists. The hearings concluded in East Harlem, with Senator Edward Kennedy and Bronx Borough President Herman Badillo decrying the fact that there were no Puerto Rican principals and only a few Puerto Rican teachers in the New York City school system.[38]

Yarborough supported bilingual legislation that focused on students whose "mother tongue is Spanish." The legislation included programs to impart knowledge of and pride about Hispanic culture and language and to bring descendants of Mexicans and Puerto Ricans into the teaching profession. The legislation was clearly designed to win political support from the Hispanic community in Texas. Yarborough's efforts resulted in the passage of the previously mentioned Bilingual Education Act of 1968.

Native Americans, along with Mexican Americans and Puerto Ricans, welcomed the idea of bilingual education. The legislation promised that their cultures and languages would be preserved by the public schools. Bilingual education, as it was conceived of in Hispanic and Native American communities, involved teaching both English and Spanish or a Native American language. Some of the Civilized Tribes in Indian Territory used bilingual methods in their schools. In addition, bilingual education existed at differing periods in Mexican-American and Puerto Rican schools. The goal is to teach students to be fluent in two languages. In addition, Mexican Americans, Puerto Ricans, and Native Americans consider bilingual education to be part of a general effort to transmit their cultural traditions to students.

By the 1980s, the two major U.S. political parties were divided over bilingual education. Traditionally, organized ethnic groups, including Mexican Americans and Puerto Ricans, were a strong force in the Democratic party. In contrast, bilingual education became a major target of attack during the Republican administrations of the 1980s and 1990s. In fact, some members of the Republican party joined a movement opposing bilingual education and supporting the adoption of English as the official language of the United States. The movement to make English the official language was led by an organization, U.S. English, founded in 1983 by S. I. Hayakawa, a former Republican senator.

In 1986, in reaction to the Reagan administration, the National Association of Bilingual Education increased its political activities and intensified its public relations efforts. In reference to S. I. Hayakawa and U.S. English, Gene T. Chavez, the president of the association, warned that "those who think this country can only tolerate one language" were motivated more by political than by educational concerns. At the same meeting, the incoming president of the organization, Chicago School Administrator Jose Gonzalez, attacked the Reagan administration and the Department of Education for entering an "unholy alliance" with right-wing groups opposing bilingual education, groups such as U.S. English, Save Our Schools, and the Heritage Foundation.[39]

Within the Reagan administration, Secretary of Education William Bennett attempted to reduce support for bilingual education by appointing opponents of it to the government's National Advisory and Coordinating Council on Bilingual Education. The new appointees expressed a preference for immersing non-English-speaking children in the English language, rather than teaching them in a bilingual context. In addition, the new appointees favored giving more power to local officials to determine programs. Of course, such a policy would undercut the power the Hispanic community had gained by working with the federal government. Originally, Hispanics had turned to the federal government for assistance because they lacked power in local politics.[40]

One of Bennett's appointees to the National Advisory and Coordinating Council on Bilingual Education, Rosalie Pedalino Porter, director of the Bilingual and English as a Second Language programs in Newton, Massachusetts, wrote a book on the controversy with the descriptive title *Forked Tongue: The Politics of Bilingual Edu-*

cation. For Porter, the politics of bilingual education involves political struggle within the educational establishment and the broader issue of cultural politics. Like other Bennett appointees, Porter rejects bilingual education which is also bicultural. She believes that language training should be geared toward providing the students with the language tools necessary for equal opportunity within the mainstream economy. But, unlike the more conservative of Bennett's appointees, she does not support attempts to make English the official language of the United States.

Porter's conclusions regarding bilingualism are a reflection of her broader views on cultural politics. She argues against bilingualism that is also bicultural because it segregates dominated communities with the least power. In her words, "The critical question is whether education policies that further the cultural identity of dominated groups at the same time enable dominated children to acquire the knowledge and skills to attain social and economic equality."[41]

Porter opposes the efforts of U.S. English because its efforts are provocative and based on anti-immigrant attitudes and threaten special programs for language minority groups. She quotes a statement by Richard Rodriguez as representing her position on attempts to enact an amendment to the Constitution making English the official language:

> What bothers me most about defenders of English comes down to a matter of tone. Too shrill. Too hostile. Too frightened. They seem to want to settle the issue of America's language, once and for all. But America must risk uncertainty if it is to remain true to its immigrant character. . . . We must remind the immigrant that there is an America already here. But we must never forget that we are an immigrant country, open to change.[42]

Despite opposition from civil rights organizations and professional organizations, including the National Association of Bilingual Education, the National Council of Teachers of English, the Linguistics Society of America, and the Modern Language Association, efforts to make English the official language continue at the state and national levels. In 1923, Nebraska made English the official state language, followed by Illinois in 1969. In 1978, Hawaii made English and Hawaiian the official state languages. Indicative of the concerns of the 1980s, between 1984 and 1988 fourteen other states made English the official state language.[43]

The major target of those supporting English as the official language is the ballot. Extensions to the 1965 Voting Rights Act granted citizens the right to voting information in their native languages. In communities where 5 percent or more of the population speak languages other than English, voting material must be provided in those languages. Supporters of English-language amendments argue that voters should be fluent in English and that naturalization procedures require a test given in English. Therefore, from their standpoint, ballots and election materials should be kept in English. On the other hand, opponents argue that election materials should be presented in native languages so that all groups will be on an equal footing with those who are fluent in English.

Besides the issue of political power, language is considered a cultural issue by Mexican Americans, Puerto Ricans, and Native Americans. A person's cultural perspective is directly related to attitudes regarding making English the official language. This connection is exemplified by Humberto Garza's comment regarding a requirement that Los Altos, California, city employees speak only English on the job: "Those council people from Los Altos should be made to understand that they are advocating their law in occupied Mexico [referring to the U.S. conquest of Mexican territory, including California]. . . . They should move back to England or learn how to speak the language of Native Americans."[44]

MULTICULTURAL EDUCATION, IMMIGRATION, AND THE CULTURE WARS

The reform atmosphere of the great civil rights movement contributed to the passage of the 1965 Immigration Act that did away with the restrictive immigration quota system of the 1924 Immigration Act. The new wave of immigration to the United States occurred at the same time that Native Americans, Mexican Americans, Puerto Ricans, and African Americans were demanding a place for their cultures in the public school curriculum. As a result of these demands and the problems posed in educating a new wave of immigrants, some educators began to advocate the teaching about a variety of cultures—multiculturalism—in the public schools.

The multiculturalism movement renewed the culture wars. Opponents of multiculturalism argued that the public schools should emphasize a single culture—traditional Anglo-American culture. In contrast to the late nineteenth and early twentieth centuries, when immigrants from southern and eastern Europe were greeted with Americanization programs designed for deculturalization and the implanting of Anglo-American values, the new immigrants were swept up into the debate over multiculturalism initiated by the civil rights movement.

Influenced by the great civil rights movement, the 1965 Immigration Act eliminated the blatantly racist and ethnocentric aspects of the 1924 Immigration Act. The results of the Army Alpha and Beta examinations administered during World War I contributed to the belief in the superior intelligence of northern Europeans. Wanting to protect the existing racial composition of the United States, the 1924 Immigration Act established an annual quota for immigration from individual countries based on the percentage that national group comprised of the total U.S. population in 1920. The openly stated purpose of the legislation was to limit immigration of nonwhite populations. Immigration to the United States sharply declined after 1924. After passage of the 1965 Immigration Act, immigration rapidly increased and by 1980 the top five sources of immigration were Mexico, Vietnam, the Philippines, Korea, and China-Taiwan.[45]

By the 1990s, as a result of the civil rights movement and the new immigration, the debate about multicultural education ranged from concerns with empowering oppressed people to creating national unity by teaching common cultural values. Originally, leaders of the multicultural movement in the 1960s and 1980s, such as James Banks, Christine Sleeter, and Carl Grant, were concerned with empowering oppressed people by integrating the history and culture of dominated groups into public school curricula and textbooks. In general, they wanted to reduce prejudice, eliminate sexism, and equalize educational opportunities.[46]

It was argued that the integration of different histories and culture into the curriculum would empower members of dominated and oppressed immigrant cultures by providing an understanding of the methods of cultural domination and by helping to build self esteem. For instance, the study of African-American, Native American, Puerto Rican, and Mexican-American history would serve the dual purpose of building self esteem and empowerment. In addition, the empowerment of women and people with disabilities would involve, in part, the inclusion of their histories and stories in textbooks and in the curriculum.

The study of a variety of cultures had an important influence on textbooks and classroom instruction in the United States. The cultural studies movement resulted in the integration of content into the curriculum that deals with dominated and immigrant cultures, women, and people with disabilities.

Many multicultural educators felt that simple integration of cultural studies into textbooks and the curriculum was not enough. Multicultural educator James Banks worried that many school districts consider content integration as the primary goal of multicultural education. He states, "The widespread belief that content integration constitutes the whole of multicultural education might . . . [cause] many teachers of subjects such as mathematics and science to view multicultural education as an endeavor primarily for social studies and language arts teachers."[47]

Banks proposed that multicultural education be considered a basic part of a student's general education, which means that all students become bilingual and all students study different cultural perspectives. In addition, multiculturalism should pervade the curriculum, including the general life of the school—bulletin boards, lunch rooms, and assemblies. In other words, all teachers and subjects should reflect a multicultural perspective.

In opposition to simply integrating the history and culture of dominated groups into the curriculum, some African-American leaders, such as Molefi Asante, demanded ethnocentric schools that would focus on the history and culture of a specific group and teach from a particular cultural perspective.[48] While Afrocentric schools gained the greatest attention, some Native Americans, Puerto Ricans, and Mexican Americans organized similar schools. The movement for ethnocentric schools, unlike the original movement for multicultural education, did not include concerns with gender, reducing prejudice, and students with disabilities.

The most popular of the ethnocentric schools associated with dominated cultures are Afrocentric. In the 1990s, public school districts in Miami, Baltimore, Detroit, Milwaukee, and New York created or considered plans for Afrocentric schools.[49] Advocates of Afrocentric education argue that they can improve a student's sense of self-worth, help students relate to the curriculum, and help students understand the causes of cultural domination.

An important concept in the argument for ethnocentric schools is cultural perspective. For instance, because African-American culture evolved in the context of slavery and later forms of segregation and racism, there developed a distrust and suspicion about the white Anglo-American Protestant tradition. Consequently, the Afrocentrist turned to other traditions. As one of the leading Afrocentrists, Molefi Asante, argued, "Afrocentrism directs us to . . . mediate on the power of our ancestors. . . . Afrocentricity is the belief in the centrality of Africans in post modern history."[50]

Therefore, teaching from an Afrocentric, Native American centered, Mexican-American centered, or Puerto Rican centered perspective creates a different view of the world as compared with an emphasis on white Anglo-American Protestant culture. In fact, according to Asante, moving away from a white Anglo-American Protestant centered curriculum will completely change a student's view of the world. Asante wrote about this new perspective: "A new consciousness invades our behavior and consequently with Afrocentricity you see the movies differently, you see other people differently, you read books differently, you see politicians differently; in fact, nothing is as it was before your consciousness."[51]

Supporting ethnocentric education, Jawanza Kunjufu argued that the inherent racism of white-dominated institutions hindered the education of African Americans. In his words, "We must develop programs and organizations to protect and develop African-American boys because a conspiracy exists to destroy African-American boys. The motive of the conspiracy is racism, specifically European-American male supremacy."[52] He proposed an educational program that will prepare African-American boys to understand their oppression and to be able to have a career. An important part of his proposal is to present strong African-American male role models to young black boys so that they can break through the conspiracy. Similar arguments can be presented for Native American, Puerto Rican, and Mexican-American centered educational programs.

During the 1980s and 1990s a sharp reaction occurred to multicultural education and the ethnocentric education advocated by dominated groups.[53] Protectors of Anglo-American culture, such as Arthur Schlesinger, Jr., argued that students should be united around a set of core values derived from white Anglo-American Protestant traditions.[54] Schlesinger, who is the author of many United States history books, argued that the institutions and culture of the United States are primarily the product of English and European values and that these core values should be the source of national unity. In his words, "The language of the new nation, its laws, its institutions, its political ideas, its literature, its customs, its precepts, its prayers, primarily derived from Britain."[55]

Historically, Schlesinger argues, the culture of the United States was unified by the common use of the English language and core values derived from this white Anglo-American Protestant tradition. These core values, he states, include mutual respect, individual rights, tolerance of differences, and individual participation in government.[56]

Similar to Schlesinger, Thomas Sobol, New York Commissioner of Education, stated his approval of a curriculum that unites different cultural groups around common values. Sobol states: "The democratic ideals and values to which we still aspire . . . the rule of law, freedom of speech, minority rights, tolerance of dissent, respect for individuals, and more—derive from British political and legal traditions."[57]

In California, State Superintendent of Education Bill Honig defended a new social studies curriculum by an appeal to the teaching of core values. Honig stated in 1991, "This country has been able to celebrate pluralism but keep some sense of the collective that holds us together. . . . Democracy has certain core ideas—freedom of speech, law, procedural rights, the way we deal with each other."[58]

Both Schlesinger, Sobol, and Honig recognized that United States history contains many examples of the violation of these principles by federal and state governments. They recognized at various times in history, federal and state governments supported slavery, committed genocide against Native Americans, and denied equal rights and opportunities to many ethnic groups. But, they argue, it was these core values that provided the impetus for correcting these wrongs. The abolition of slavery, the extension of political rights to women, and the civil rights campaigns by African Americans, Mexican Americans, Native Americans, Puerto Ricans, and Asian Americans reflect these core values. These civil rights movements, according the Schlesinger, were based on the core values of the white Anglo-Saxon Protestant tradition.[59]

Given this perspective, it is hardly surprising that those calling for the teaching of core values would object to the forms of ethnocentric education, particularly, Afrocentric education, advocated by dominated groups. Schlesinger attacked Afrocentric education for distorting the importance of Africa in the development of Western traditions and in the development of African-American culture. Because of the variety of African cultures from which African Americans are descended, Schlesinger argued, it is hard to identify a common African heritage for African Americans. In addition, many African cultures are more oppressive than the white Anglo-American Protestant culture as proven by the fact that slavery continued in Africa for many years after it was abolished in the United States.[60]

In addition, Schlesinger rejected the idea of teaching history for the purpose of building a sense of self-worth among children. In his words, "The deeper reason for the Afrocentric campaign lies in the theory that the purpose of history in the schools is essentially therapeutic: to build a sense of self-worth among minority children."[61] With regard to the teaching of the history of Africa, Schlesinger rejected the direct connection between African heritage and African-American culture and dismisses the practice with the statement: "There is little evidence, however, that such invention of tradition is much more than a pastime of a few angry, ambitious, and perhaps despairing zealots and hustlers."[62]

The culture wars of the late twentieth century reflect the centuries-old effort to make English and Anglo-American Protestant culture the unifying language and culture of the United States. Originating in the sense of cultural superiority brought to North America by English colonists and emerging during cultural wars throughout U.S. history, the attempt to make Anglo-American culture the dominant culture of the United States was seriously challenged by the great civil rights movement and the new immigration.

NOTES

1. Arthur M. Schlesinger Jr., *The Disuniting of America* (Knoxville, TN: Whittle Direct Books, 1991), p. 8.
2. *Brown et al.* v. *Board of Education of Topeka et al.* (1954), reprinted in Albert P. Blaustein and Clarence C. Ferguson, Jr., *Desegregation and the Law* (New Brunswick, NJ: Rutgers University Press, 1957), pp. 273–282.
3. "The Effects of Segregation and the Consequences of Desegregation: A Social Science Statement," appendix to Appellants' Brief filed in the

School Segregation Cases in the Supreme Court of the United States, October term, 1952, in John Bracey, August Meier, and Elliott Rudwick, eds., *The Afro-Americans: Selected Documents* (Boston: Allyn & Bacon, 1972), pp. 661–671.

4. Ibid.
5. Gunnar Myrdal, *An American Dilemma: The Negro Problem and Modern Democracy* (New York: Harper & Row, 1944), pp. lxxii–lxxiii.
6. Martin Luther King, Jr., *Stride Toward Freedom: The Montgomery Story* (New York: Harper & Row, 1958), p. 91.
7. Ibid., pp. 94–97.
8. Francis Paul Prucha, *The Indians in American Society: From Revolutionary War to the Present* (Berkeley: University of California Press, 1985), p. 70.
9. Ibid., pp. 72–75.
10. Ibid., p. 74.
11. Jon Reyhner and Jeanne Eder, *A History of Indian Education* (Billings: Eastern Montana College, 1989), pp. 125–126.
12. Ibid., p. 126.
13. Prucha, *Indians in American Society*, p. 82.
14. Ibid., p. 83.
15. U.S. Congress, Senate Committee on Labor and Public Welfare, *Indian Education: A National Tragedy—A National Challenge*, 91st Cong., 1st Sess. (Washington, D.C.: U.S. Government Printing Office, 1969), p. 9.
16. Ibid., p. 106.
17. Reyhner and Eder, *History of Indian Education*, pp. 132–135.
18. "Indian Education Act, June 23, 1972," in Francis Paul Prucha, ed., *Documents of United States Indian Policy* (Lincoln: University of Nebraska Press, 1990), pp. 263–264.
19. "Student Rights and Due Process Procedures, October 11, 1974," in Prucha, *Documents*, p. 271.
20. Ibid.
21. "Indian Self-Determination and Education Assistance Act, January 4, 1975," in Prucha, *Documents*, p. 274.
22. "Tribally Controlled Schools Act of 1988," in Prucha, *Documents*, pp. 314–315.
23. "American Indian Religious Freedom, August 11, 1978," in Prucha, *Documents*, pp. 288–289.
24. Reyhner and Eder, *History of Indian Education*, p. 137.
25. Ibid., p. 126.
26. Quoted in Ibid., p. 128.
27. Ibid., pp. 127–129. Also see Gilbert G. Gonzalez, *Chicano Education in the Era of Segregation* (Philadelphia: Balch Institute Press, 1990), pp. 147–156.
28. Guadalupe San Miguel, Jr., *"Let All of Them Take Heed": Mexican Ameri-*

cans and the Campaign for Educational Equality in Texas, 1910–1981 (Austin: University of Texas Press, 1987), pp. 123–124.
29. Ibid., p. 125.
30. Charles Wollenberg, *All Deliberate Speed: Segregation and Exclusion in California Schools, 1855–1975* (Berkeley: University of California Press, 1976), p. 134.
31. San Miguel, *"Let All of Them Take Heed,"* pp. 169–173.
32. Ibid., pp. 173–174.
33. Ibid., pp. 177–179.
34. Wollenberg, *All Deliberate Speed*, pp. 134–135.
35. San Miguel, *"Let All of Them Take Heed,"* p. 168.
36. Ibid.
37. Hugh Davis Graham, *Uncertain Triumph: Federal Educational Policy in the Kennedy and Johnson Years* (Chapel Hill: University of North Carolina Press, 1984), p. 155.
38. Ibid., p. 156.
39. James Crawford, "Bilingual Educators Seeking Strategies to Counter Attacks," *Education Week*, Vol. 5, No. 28 (April 9, 1986), pp. 1, 9.
40. James Crawford, "Administration Panel Praises Bennett's Bilingual-Education Stance," *Education Week*, Vol. 5, No. 28 (April 9, 1986), p. 9.
41. Rosalie Pedalino Porter, *Forked Tongue: The Politics of Bilingual Education* (New York: Basic Books, 1990), p. 188.
42. Ibid., pp. 219–220.
43. Ibid., pp. 210–211.
44. Quoted in Ibid., p. 216.
45. David Reimers, *Still the Golden Door: The Third World Comes to America* (New York: Columbia University Press, 1985).
46. See James Banks, "Multicultural Education: Historical Development, Dimensions, and Practice," *Review of Research in Education 19*, edited by Linda Darling-Hammond (Washington, D.C.: American Educational Research Association, 1993), pp. 3–50; and Sonia Nieto, *Affirming Diversity: The Sociopolitical Context of Multicultural Education* (White Plains, NY: Longman Inc., 1992).
47. Banks, p. 5.
48. For instance, see Molefi Kete Asante, *Afrocentricity* (Trenton, NJ: Africa World Press, 1988).
49. Kevin Brown, "Do African American Males Need Race and Gender Segregated Education?: An Educator's Perspective and a Legal Perspective," in *The New Politics of Race and Gender*, edited by Catherine Marshall (Washington, D.C.: Falmer Press, 1993), p. 107.
50. Asante, *Afrocentricity*, pp. 4–5.
51. Asante, *Afrocentricity*, p. 7.
52. Jawanza Kunjufu, *Countering the Conspiracy to Destroy Black Boys* (Chicago: African American Images, 1985), p. 32.

53. A good case study of this reaction in California and Texas is Catherine Cornbleth and Detter Waugh's *The Great Speckled Bird: Multicultural Politics and Education Policy Making* (New York: St. Martin's Press, 1995).
54. See Arthur M. Schlesinger, Jr., *The Disuniting of America* (Knoxville, TN: Whittle Direct Books, 1991).
55. Ibid., p. 8.
56. Ibid., p. 80.
57. Thomas Sobol, "Revising the New York State Social Studies Curriculum," *Teachers College Record*, Vol. 95, No. 1 (Winter 1993), p. 266.
58. Caroline B. Cody, Arthur Woodward, and David L. Elliot, "Race, Ideology and the Battle Over the Curriculum," in *The New Politics of Race and Gender*, edited by Catherine Marshall (Washington, D.C.: Falmer Press, 1993), p. 55.
59. Schlesinger, *Disuniting*, p. 15.
60. Ibid., pp. 40–55.
61. Ibid., p. 43.
62. Ibid., p. 47.

Index